D0886635

Carole Mallory

Mallory, Carole.
Loving Mailer / Carole Mallory.
p. cm.
ISBN-13: 978-1-60747-715-0 (hc)
ISBN-10: 1-60747-715-7 (hc)
1. Mailer, Norman--Relations with women. 2. Authors, American--20th century--Biography. 3. Mallory, Carole. 4. Mistresses--United States--Biography. I. Title.
PS3525.A4152Z763 2010
813'.54--dc22
[B]

2010000646

Jacket & Book Design by Rick Crane

Printed in the United States of America

Phoenix Books, Inc.
9465 Wilshire Boulevard, Suite 840
Beverly Hills, CA 90212

10 9 8 7 6 5 4 3 2 1

Dedication

To the memory of my loving mother, Laura "Lulu" Lengel Wagner, who often asked what I saw in Norman, and for Kenny.

Prologue

I wanted to have sex with Warren Beatty to forget.

"Good evening. Hotel Carlyle."

"Warren Beatty, please."

"Who's calling Mr. Beatty?"

"Mrs. Ronald Mallory."

"I'll see if he's taking calls."

"What a pleasant surprise," Warren purred. "To what do I owe this pleasure, Mrs. Mallory?"

"Do you want to fuck?" I said sternly.

"I'll be right over."

Within twenty minutes Warren was at my door. He did not enter.

For a long time he stood in the entrance staring at me. I prayed that he wouldn't notice my trembling. I meant business and wanted to grow up—to learn to have sex, not to feel guilty, not to fall in love, to accept Warren for what he led me to believe he was—a great lover—and not to want anything in return. No wedding rings, no engraved invitations, no bottles or diapers to change, no checking out in-laws, no joint bank accounts, no dinner invitations, no two-car garages, no answers, no questions. But I did want to forget my father's suffering.

"Come in," I said.

"I intend to," he said. He walked slowly around the living room, inspecting my furniture.

"Do you want a drink?"

"I don't drink," he said.

Well, I did. I poured myself a second glass of wine.

Warren paused by a Lucite barstool, stared at it, then said, "We're going to Elaine's."

"Great," I said.

"Bob Altman will be joining us. Hope you don't mind. Thought you might like to meet him. He directs lots of films," Warren said to a painting, then turned to me.

"I'm a model, Warren. Not an actress," I said to my wineglass.

"Maybe one day you'll change your mind." Slowly he gestured toward the door. "Shall we?" Warren did everything slowly.

When we walked into Elaine's, the Red Sea parted again. I passed that coterie of male writers I had been drinking with on many a night. I felt stares and heard whispers.

Bob Altman had rosy cheeks and a chuckle that reminded me of St. Nick. By his side was a silver ice bucket filled with champagne. Altman had invited Warren to dinner to try to talk him into starring in another film now that *McCabe & Mrs. Miller,* which had been directed by Altman and starred Warren, had just been released. It was spring of 1971.

Altman ordered more Dom Perignon.

I drank enough for Warren, and myself. Warren was amazing. A superstar who didn't drink Dom Perignon. Warren ate only healthy foods. No bread, butter, or meat. Fresh vegetables cooked al dente. Hearty veggies to make a hearty lover? I wasn't so sure. Underneath the table he began playing with my garters.

I felt good with Warren, though I was nervous. I could feel his power, and in a strange way I felt safe. If I lost my nerve to have sex with him, I could always reject him. I was better at rejecting men than making love to them.

When we walked out of Elaine's, I felt like a long shot in the Derby. I could feel the bets being placed.

Our cab took us to the Sherry-Netherland, where Bob Altman had a suite.

"He wants to talk about his next film," Warren said and yawned.

"Why go?"

"I want him to watch over the distribution of *McCabe*. Opened yesterday."

At the Sherry, Altman pressured Warren, and Warren pressured Altman.

I wanted to say I had walked out of *McCabe & Mrs. Miller*. Instead I reached for more champagne.

Back in the cab Warren asked, "Do you mind driving by Loew's on 86th Street? I want to check out the line for *McCabe*."

"Why?" I asked.

"It's important that there's a sizable crowd at this hour. The film opened yesterday, and if it's going to be a hit...," he said, murmuring as he pulled me into his arms and kissed me. His lips moved with experience. Gently he opened his mouth on mine.

For thirty blocks we embraced. My shirt was down to my waist where it met my skirt.

His left hand on my breast. His right hand between my thighs.

The driver looked back. Then ahead. Then back.

Warren didn't care.

"Loew's 86th," the driver said, looking back.

Warren didn't look up. We lay sprawled on the backseat. "333 East 69th," said Warren, giving my address in his deep, commanding tone. "It's what you want, isn't it, baby?"

I hated to be called "baby." I was sure men used it—especially stars—when they couldn't remember a woman's name.

"333 East 69th," the driver said again, turning. He stared. A long time. Warren handed me my panties, then stepped out of the cab, zipping his fly.

The doorman's eyes widened. "Good evening, Mrs. Mallory."

Warren followed me to the elevator then pressed the button. "Well, what has happened to Mr. Mallory, Mrs. Mallory?"

I wanted to slug him. Instead I smiled. "Time for a change," I said, wondering why women were respected when virgins and men respected when lovers. At twenty-nine, I was going to find out.

Inside my apartment, the superstar began once again to inspect my furniture. Did he have a fetish? He removed his jacket and opened his shirt.

"I like your husband. He seems like a nice guy," Warren said.

"Oh, really...thanks," I said, tempted to say, "Want to pay his bills?"

Warren removed the candelabra from my dining table.

I decided to shut him out with another glass of wine. On our date Warren had held my chair at the table, my elbow when walking. Now, I was having to put up with a lot of crap to find out what Warren Beatty, superstar, was like in bed. I hope he'll be worth it, I thought, walking toward the bathroom. When I returned to the living room, he was fiddling with my Lucite bar stool. It was a contemporary Italian design and swiveled horizontally, like a seat at a soda fountain.

"I sure like this chair," he said, his voice a purr. "I want to show you something. We're going to have a good time. Sit," he said, as though I were on a leash.

I was.

Thank God we were beginning, and I wouldn't have to listen to him anymore.

Warren stared at me for a long time then gently began kissing me. Suddenly, another command. "Undress. Leave your garters on. And your stockings and shoes."

I was embarrassed. I frowned.

"You heard me," he said.

I did as I was told, like a good little bad girl. I felt awkward with my body, even though photographers told me it was beautiful. My entire family was filled with shame about their bodies. I had never seen my mother naked. I finished my wine. Quickly.

"My, you are a true brunette, Mrs. Mallory," he said, staring long and hard.

Now I knew how Little Red Riding Hood felt.

"Hold tight," he said, smiling slightly as he stood over me. "We're about to begin." Delicately, he slipped the fingers of his right hand one by one into my mouth. "Come on. Make them wet. Real wet. Suck them." Then his fingers were all over me. "You won't forget tonight," he said. "You like this, don't you?" His voice a hum. He knelt at the base of the barstool and began moving it back and forth as he kissed me.

I held his head. Yanked his hair. Let out a cry.

Warren looked into my eyes. His expression had passion I had never seen in his movies. His purring voice, his hypnotic stare, made him more potent than any drug I had ever had. His confidence bolstered me. He wouldn't waste his time if he didn't think I could be a good lover too. He believed in my sexuality and was forcing me to believe in it as well. Tenderly he held me, then whispered, "You liked that, didn't you?"

There was no need to answer. I opened my eyes to a completely naked Warren Beatty. Built just right. Just what my fantasies had ordered.

Dripping with perspiration, I was about to slip off the barstool when he stopped me. "I'm not through with you yet, or this chair." He was inside me. He was staring into my eyes. "Touch yourself."

"No."

"I told you what I wanted from you. Do it!" he ordered.

I began to love my body. Warren's voice and stare melted my shame. I felt good. Light-headed. Free. Complete. Okay. And right. Very right. Suddenly I cried out. Some part of me felt slaughtered.

He held me. We fell to the floor, lost in time. "Easy, girl, easy."

After a long silence, I said, "Thanks, Warren, I needed that."

"You sure did. Hasn't anyone made love to you right? You don't have to answer that."

Soon Warren returned to the bathroom. The faucet ran for some time. Warren was clean. Squeaky clean.

I refreshed his water with ice cubes then slipped into the bathroom. No longer caring what I looked like. I was beginning to feel like a star myself.

Now Warren was surveying my round, white Formica dining table. "That's some chair," he said with a half smile.

"It cost seven hundred dollars. It was worth it."

"Yeah, I like this table too. Get me Vaseline."

I traipsed back to the bathroom, grabbed the Vaseline, and threw on an old kimono. When I returned from my errand, he shouted, "Why are you wearing that thing?"

"I thought we'd talk a bit."

"Take it off!"

"Why?"

"Take it off! You heard me!"

I obeyed.

"And take off that garter belt. We're through with that. Get on the table. On all fours. Here." Warren handed me a joint. It was the first time I'd had marijuana. After three puffs, I felt free with my body, and willing to do what Warren wanted.

He walked around the table, holding a lighted Rigaud candle. He inspected my body, inch by every candlelight inch, like he had inspected my furniture. "What a beauty you are, Mrs. Mallory," he said. "This will be another surprise. A real treat."

I took two more puffs from the joint.

"Do exactly what I tell you. Relax," he said sternly. "You're made for this. You'll never forget it or me."

I could feel myself ripping off years of sexual guilt. Those Pennsylvania Dutch hex signs in Shoemakersville. Fear, erased. "Come on. You're the stud," I heard myself shout. "Show me!"

"You're made for fucking. With a body like this. That's all you should do. And I'm going to do it. Until you want no one else. Nobody can fuck you like I can. No one. Rejecting me all those times. You cunt. You beautiful cunt. I'll show you. Here it is, baby. For you. Take it. See if you can."

I screamed. Warren put his hand over my mouth.

Sex had never felt like this. I wanted more orgasms like this.

I wanted to see Warren again. That wasn't part of my bargain. I was determined not to fall in love with a superstar reputed to exploit women.

Warren held me. We sank onto the tabletop, rolled over, and faced the ceiling. Our bodies entwined.

"You're something else, Mrs. Mallory."

"Would you stop that 'Mrs. Mallory'?"

For some time we listened to Carole King.

Warren went back into the bathroom. When he returned, he sat by the cocktail table, turning Ron's round mercury sculpture in his hands. "I like your husband's work. It's erotic."

I went into the bathroom, bothered by Warren's references to my soon-to-be ex-husband. Grabbing a faded, yellow, terry cloth robe, I wrapped it around me and came back out.

Warren was in the bedroom, staring at a topless photograph of me, seated in the desert.

"Who was this for?" he asked.

"Some Japanese car."

"Great."

As he studied my partially naked body in the photo, I studied his completely naked body on the bed. His bottom was flat. Not much to it. His humanness, I thought.

The silence was making me nervous. I pulled my robe around me and said, "Warren, you have a wonderful body."

"Played football in high school."

"What position?"

Warren's sense of humor was minimal. He didn't respond. He continued to look at my picture.

"The first man I ever had sex with is today one of the coaches for the Pittsburgh Stee…"

"Don't tell me about your old fucks, baby," he said, again the general. He sat on the edge of the bed. "Kiss me. AND TAKE THAT SILLY ROBE OFF…. *WHERE DO YOU KEEP GETTING THEM?* Don't ever put one on again when I'm around."

By now I was immune to his bellowing.

"Just be yourself. Anything you do will be fine," he whispered, no longer the tyrant. His body had taken on new life. (All those fresh vegetables?) His expression, sweet and dreamy-eyed. I felt he was beginning to like me, but didn't want me to know.

"You're doing fine, Carole," he said softly.

Yep, I was in love with Warren Beatty. Though he ridiculed what I said, he didn't ridicule my sexuality.

"Sit on me," he said, lifting me onto him. "You know you're the most beautiful woman I've ever seen, other than those Hollywood beauties."

I was going to accept Warren *and* his lines, and love him. I wasn't the only one who wanted to fuck Warren Beatty, and I wasn't going to be ashamed for having this pleasure. (Some part of my father would be proud of me—I could still hear Daddy saying, "If you're going to do something, do it right and with the very best.") Having an orgasm with Warren was like being freed from solitary and the guilt from the past. I wanted to scream, "Leave me, go. Let me live. I don't want to love you. I don't want to need you. You'll hurt me." Suddenly I let out a wail.

Warren pushed me onto the bed and held a pillow over my head. I pounded him with my fists. "Easy, easy," he said.

I thrashed about under the pillow.

Then we lay in bed in silence. Carol King sang.

"You love to come, don't you?" he said. "I don't think I've ever been with a woman that emotional. Do you always make sounds like that?"

I didn't answer.

Then he went back into the bathroom while I went into the kitchen. More wine. When he returned, spanking clean once more, he opened the fridge and pulled out a bunch of grapes. "I'm tired," he said. He grabbed my waist. "I think I'd like to go to bed now. Would you?"

"Yes."

"Shall we?"

Still naked, he began walking toward the bedroom.

"Warren, I think you should go."

He turned. His face had flushed. "Are you crazy?" His impenetrable cool had shattered.

I was trying to be grown-up. If he really wanted me, he could always call tomorrow.

"Warren, you got what you came for. What more do you want?" I said. I was trying to hide my tears.

"I want to stay with you," he said sincerely. (Sincerity was not his strong card, but he had never sounded more sincere.) "Let me love you. You want that too."

"Warren, thanks for the fuck," I said, afraid if he held me, I'd melt in his arms and become that little girl I really was. I had what I wanted. To forget my pain for a few hours.

Quickly he dressed. In a clear voice he said, "You'll regret this. One day you'll want me to make love to you." Then he slammed the door in my face.

Twelve years later, after love affairs with many movie stars and now sober, I longed for a man who could not only stimulate me sexually but with whom I could talk about a wide variety of subjects. What this man looked like was less important than what he said. Most important was that he not only appreciate looking at me but also value listening to me. I had felt like an object to many of the stars with whom I had made love. Oh, they would flatter me endlessly, but exchanging meaningful conversations with them was rare. The irony was that while my intelligence was not being taken seriously, I was the one feeling the stars were empty vessels. These stars may have demeaned me, but I was disappointed in them. I wanted to find someone not intellectually boring. I longed for a melding of the minds more than a joining of the bodies. I wanted a long-term relationship with somebody I could talk to and exchange ideas with and feel close to on many levels. Someone who would have something all of the other stars did not have. I longed for a relationship where we would stimulate each other intellectually.

I longed for a love affair with a genius.

Chapter 1

It all began one snowy evening in December 1983 at Elaine's Restaurant on Manhattan's Upper East Side.

On our first date, Buzz Farber, a writer, talked of nothing but Norman Mailer. I had been lonely for my old friends from the early seventies. I had been living in Hollywood since that cursed night in 1975 when I flew away from my fiancé Claude Picasso in Paris because he would not set a wedding date.

New York was home. I had fond memories of my life here. Life as a supermodel, being on covers of magazines, acting in a groundbreaking movie, *Stepford Wives*, (and then almost becoming a Stepford wife again with Claude Picasso). Life with my husband, Ronald Mallory, the successful sculptor, had been fun. Ron had introduced me to New York's art world and Andy Warhol, Richard Lindner, Roy Lichtenstein, and Marc Rothko, who had come to our wedding. In 1968 Ron introduced me to Elaine's where we would meet his collectors, photographers, models, magazine editors, celebrities, and writers.

Going to Elaine's was a way to run into these friends. On a break from acting assignments, I was visiting New York for a few weeks.

Suddenly Norman Mailer entered the literary haunt. "Excuse me, I've got to talk to Norman," Buzz said, bolting toward Norman's table.

I'd heard about Mailer, a womanizer of the worst sort. Buzz had better not be trying to fix me up. In Hollywood it was the casting couch. Was it like that in publishing? "I'll edit your writing and show it to my publisher?"

I turned around to catch a glimpse of Norman, but the restaurant was too crowded. While stirring my fettuccini and listening to Ray Charles on the jukebox, I wondered why Georgia wasn't on my mind instead of Norman Mailer?

I wanted to be a writer. That's why.

Someone touched my shoulder. "Would you like to meet Norman?" Buzz said, standing behind me.

"Why not?" I said, feigning indifference. Some twenty years ago hadn't Mailer stabbed one of his wives during an alcoholic blackout? I'd read he'd gotten off by claiming a crime of passion.

Surely Mailer had stopped drinking by now.

As Buzz and I approached Norman's table, I thought maybe Norman and I could talk about how much better life is sober.

Before looking at Norman, I looked at what he was drinking. A whiskey sour.

Dear God! Hadn't anyone tried to help this poor man? Then I noticed everyone in Norman's party was drinking.

Norman stood, tugged at the vest of his navy pinstriped suit and pushed out his lower lip. "Buzz told me you're from Hollywood," he said, shaking my hand. His eyes were a Paul Newman blue. His voice, a magnificent baritone like my father's. He was shorter than five-foot-six-and-a-half-inch me and had a gentle-looking face, jovial expression, and curly white hair. How could this man have stabbed a woman, I thought—then gazed at the whiskey sour he embraced. Like me, Norman was allergic to alcohol, I was sure.

"Well, actually, I'm from Philadelphia," I said.

"In Philly they sell the hole in the doughnut."

"In New York don't they sell the hole in the bagel?"

"In Brooklyn," Norman said, smiling. "Are you a comedian?"

"An actress," I said, too embarrassed to tell Norman that I was writing.

"Sit," he said as Buzz pulled up a chair and placed it by Norman's side. Buzz then introduced me to Norman's wife, Norris Church, and Mr. and Mrs. Ivan Fisher, Norman's lawyer and his wife. Norris Church was a tall woman who wore bright red lipstick that stood out against her alabaster skin. She must be a model, I thought, when I noticed her well-manicured makeup and beauty. Perhaps she just finished work. When I modeled, I would leave my makeup on and then go out to dinner.

"Would you like a drink?" Norman asked.

"A Diet Coke, thanks. I don't drink. I'm an alcoholic," I said, wanting to hear his response.

"Didn't you find abstaining from drink tough the first year?" he asked.

I studied Norman's sad, glassy eyes. "I needed my support group. Couldn't have done it alone."

"I tried no drink for a year, but the parties got boring." Norman laughed.

Nothing was funny, I thought.

"Parties are boring," I said.

Norman was giving signals. None of these people could hear he wanted help. Why? Because they were all drinking alcohol too.

"I always write sober. Tennessee Williams died from swallowing the cap of his pill bottle. Probably my insides will fall out." Norman paused as he drank more of his whiskey sour. "Don't some men have trouble getting erections when they take the pledge?"

"It just takes time." I paused. "And practice."

Norman laughed.

"I'll bet drunken sex is better," Ivan Fisher said, wineglass in hand.

Norman ignored Fisher's comment, lowered his voice and said, sotto voce, "Did you know the male sperm is not as strong as the female egg; therefore, one must have a lot of sex to make a male baby?"

"Does that mean male sperm is fragile and feminine?" I asked.

"You could call it that. Masculine sex makes a girl and feminine sex makes a boy," Norman said, downing his drink. "Buzz told me you're an actress. Have you been in any films I might have seen?"

"*Stepford Wives. Looking for Mr. Goodbar*."

"*Goodbar*. Good film." Norman cleared his throat. "Was just on TV. What part did you play?"

"I was in the orgy with Tuesday Weld."

"I remember you." Norman chuckled. His belly shook as he clasped his pudgy fingers over his tight vest. "How was Richard Brooks as a director?"

"Tuesday Weld really directed. He directed traffic."

"What's it like filming an orgy?" Norman asked, amused.

"Hard work. Everyone was covered in black tape."

"Must hurt when they pull it off."

I knew this talk was making an impression on Norman. The wrong kind. Though I had been sober four years, my self-worth was still low. Not to worry, I told myself. Norman's gentlemanly and fatherly presence made it impossible to believe that he was still the womanizer. Maybe I was trying to come on to him a bit. He was thoroughly charming and fun to tease. I was drawn to his sense of humor.

"I've got some briefs to read," Fisher said. "You and Buzz want a lift?"

"Thanks, Ivan, but we'll take a cab," said Buzz, who had talked nonstop when we were together, but when Norman and I began our exchange, everyone listened. Norman liked to hold court.

Buzz turned to Norman. "*Esquire* took Carole on a date," Buzz said. "Remember those articles, Norman? Interviews with beautiful actresses? Diana Ross. Susan Sarandon."

Was Buzz trying to sell me to Norman, I wondered? Why the promotion of my résumé?

"Sure," Norman said. "Lee Eisenberg's writing. What was the occasion?"

"Carole's been on lots of magazine covers and…." Buzz continued his hard sell.

"A few," I said. "I was promoting a film I had been in called *Take This Job and Shove It*."

"Some days I'd like to do that," Norman said, throwing his napkin on the table.

"Shall we?" Fisher said, signaling departure.

When we returned to our table, I thought about Norman Mailer. He was such a sweet man. Cute. Even though he was a bit old. I wondered what he thought of me?

When Buzz walked me to my door, he said, "Norman liked you. If he doesn't like my dates, he insults them. He doesn't like most of my dates."

Norman seemed a little peculiar. He was handsome in an elder-statesman way. I hoped we'd meet again.

Chapter 2

A few weeks after meeting Norman, I read in the *New York Times* that he would be speaking at the Thalia at a retrospective of his film work. The event was sold out; nevertheless, during January's worst snowstorm, I trudged to the old movie house on West 96th Street. A SOLD OUT sign hung in the window of the dimly lit box office. It was 8:00 p.m.

"Do you have one ticket?" I asked anyway.

"You're in luck," the man said. "You get the last seat."

Destiny. I was meant to meet Norman again.

The theater was packed. I squeezed into a middle row of the tiny movie house.

Wearing a navy pullover with patches over the elbows, a white shirt, and khakis, Norman stood center stage and introduced himself. The audience cheered and whistled. A few booed good-naturedly.

"Boo to you, too," Norman said, chuckling. He held his belly with both hands as though he were insulating himself from the crowd and spoke about his films: *Wild 90, Beyond the Law*. "In *Maidstone* when I hit Rip Torn with the hammer, that scene was improvisation. Blood kept running out of his nose, but we kept filming. He didn't speak to me for years, but judge for yourselves the results."

The audience hooted. Norman glowed, eager to please his fans. After interminable hours of watching each of his films and listening to his lectures, I was exhausted by him. Much of the audience had walked out. Norman would not leave the stage.

"Any more questions?" he asked, until no one dared to raise a hand. His insatiable need for attention showed a narcissistic streak, yet his patience and willingness to share his creativity showed a generosity of spirit. Norman's character had so many contradictions.

Throughout the evening I had been trying to concoct a way to meet Norman again. He had to read my manuscript—my autobiography focusing on my life in Hollywood. I had to make this happen. How? Appeal to his wit. He likes to and needs to laugh. There's so much tragedy to this man. Be light. Sunshine. No pressure. *Oh, how do I find the nerve to write the winner of two Pulitzer Prizes, two National Book Awards, and author of twenty-five books?* I thought, rummaging through my handbag for paper and pen. Out of my Filofax, I tore a blank page and scribbled a few sentences.

"Dear Mr. Mailer, We met at Elaine's a few weeks ago with Buzz Farber. Consider this note valid for one cheeseburger at the Lenox Hill Coffee Shop. 74th & Lex. Tomorrow at 11 a.m. Kindly RSVP." And I wrote my number.

What a dumb note. But I couldn't tell him I'd written something I wanted him to read. How would I get this note to him?

Somewhere after midnight Norman said, "If any of you have further questions, I'll be in the back of the theater for a few minutes. Thank you for coming."

I stayed in my seat until most of the audience left and kept my eyes on Norman. The rear of the theater was dark, but I made my way along with the crowd and stood on the edge of a circle of die-hard fans quizzing Norman. After half an hour, a few people remained. It was time. I inhaled, grabbed my note, and plunged forward, introducing myself.

"I remember you," Norman said. His face brightened.

"Could I invite you to brunch tomorrow?" I said. "You see, I leave town in two days." My legs trembled. My voice, almost a whine.

Norman scanned my note and smiled. "I'll meet you at eleven. If I can't make it, I'll call."

"Thanks for the great evening," I said, then turned around and hurried out of the theater. How could I have done such a brazen thing?

I remembered the time before my father got sick. He drove into a nudist camp to tease my mother, who was Pennsylvania Dutch. "Pulling her leg" or "getting her goat" he used to call it. My father parked the car right in the middle of a wooded area where naked bathers were returning from the lake.

"Do you want me to get a divorce, Herb?" Mother shouted while my sister and I crouched down in the backseat and giggled as we peered every so often out the window at the nudists.

I loved my father for this. For his defiance of public opinion. He sold fire insurance, and the day after there had been a fire on the block, my father would knock on the neighbors' doors and ask if they wanted fire insurance.

Mother would scold him about this, but he would just do it again.

My father would have been proud of what I had done. Now I had to organize my writings and thoughts for Norman. Out of the five hundred pages, what did I want him to read? Would he really show up?

I certainly hoped so. He was so funny. Charming. He reminded me of my father. He was old enough to be my father. Pity he was married. Didn't matter because he wasn't my type. Stay focused on the writing, I told myself as I walked out of the Thalia into the snowy night on the Upper West Side of Manhattan. I was alone and felt good. The snow was deep. The stars bright. And I was about to make a new friend. A writer. A very good writer. A genius.

Chapter 3

At 11:15 Norman pushed through the door of the Lenox Hill Coffee Shop, clapping his mittens together to shake off the snow. He seemed happy to see me. Of course. Bet he thought we were going to have sex. I had told him that I was in the orgy in *Goodbar*, then invited him to lunch. I yanked my bulky turtleneck to my chin. Still I couldn't tell him my intentions and hid my manuscript under my coat on the booth next to me. I was surprised at how good he looked. More youthful than the other two times I had seen him. So what if he had wanted to have sex. I was used to men reacting to me like that. Besides, how did I know what he was thinking? Here was a writer I could talk to. About writing. And he wasn't just any writer. He was a great writer. I realized I felt good seeing him again and was flattered that he showed up.

Norman pulled off his red ski cap, unzipped his blue nylon parka, and sat facing me. Overweight, he had trouble sliding his tummy under the table. "Have you been waiting long?" he asked.

"No," I said, placing a napkin over my eggs. I didn't think he would show up.

"I've been at the gym."

"Which one?" I asked.

"14th Street. Uptown."

"Uptown?" I laughed.

"Sure. To me it's uptown. I live in Brooklyn."

"What do you do at the gym?"

"Box. I'm a boxer."

"I loved *The Fight*."

"A fan, I see," he said, rubbing his hands together. He signaled the waitress for a coffee. "Do you work out?"

"I swim at a gym in L.A."

"I'm getting old. My knees hurt. When I don't feel up to the ring, I walk forty blocks a day. What did you want to see me about?" he asked without innuendo. Impressed by his forthrightness, I remained the coward. My hand on my hidden manuscript.

Bracing myself for his sudden exit, I looked down at my soggy scrambled eggs and said, "Would you look at something I've written?"

"Sure," he said. His eyes sparkled. "Where is it?"

Suddenly I felt comfortable with Norman.

From under my coat I pulled out the five hundred pages, bound in a plastic cover. My face, crimson like its cover.

"Wow!" Norman said. "Let me see. I'll open it to wherever. Skim. That's as good a way as any. Why the title? *Picasso Loves Me*?"

"A writer suggested it. Harvey Miller, who wrote *Private Benjamin*. Do you know him?"

"No. Good film, but don't take advice from every writer."

"Most of it's about my engagement to Claude Picasso and the family."

"The family." Norman chuckled. His exuberance was captivating and contagious. Childlike. He reminded me of a giant teddy bear in need of a cuddle. "Some family. Well, that's interesting. The title isn't. Grandiose. Good God."

"It's just a working title," I said, embarrassed.

The waitress appeared and took our order. Cheeseburger for Norman and scrambled eggs for me.

Norman held my manuscript between his palms and banged its binder on the table, releasing it as the pages opened. "This is how I do it. Like the *I Ching*. I never read a writer's rough work from the beginning."

Though Norman could embellish the truth, while he read his eyes were incapable of deception. I would later learn that if I wanted to know what Norman meant, I would have to watch him while listening to him. This made phone calls a problem because I could not see Norman's expression. I soon learned that his voice would become thin and high, or he would adopt a Texas accent when he segued into fiction. Norman's favorite phrase for dodging confrontation would be, "I'll tell you about it when I see you." He rarely would.

Norman began to read the chapter on Picasso. His lips moved while his body bobbed back and forth. "You must learn to read your work aloud. Women have a tendency to explain or to justify an action."

Women, I wondered. What's gender got to do with it? "I know I do," I said. "But I don't know when I'm doing it."

"Takes time. Distance. Now I will pick something of interest to me." Norman opened to the chapter on Warren Beatty. *Why that chapter?* I thought.

As Norman turned the pages, he laughed. "That's good! That's funny because of the word 'sternly'. You've written, 'Relax, Warren said sternly.' If 'sternly' weren't there, it wouldn't be funny." (This from the man who would later tell me to eliminate all adverbs.) Norman laughed again. He liked to laugh at his own jokes. He read all twenty-six pages of the chapter without looking up. I wondered if he had an erection. He seemed fascinated with Warren Beatty—or was it my writing, or was it what was happening on the page? When Norman liked a certain passage, he pounded the table with his fist. Peeking under the booth, I caught his foot moving in rhythm with his body and his lips.

When Norman read my work, I felt sexual. I was revealing secrets. He was reading hidden thoughts. His acceptance of my words was helping me to accept myself. Then, I thought, he's a married man. Stop justifying your feelings.

After Norman finished the chapter, he closed the book and said, "You'll get this published, and you'll be rich and famous, and no star will fuck you again." He sipped his coffee. "They'll be afraid of you."

"You mean you won't?" I said defiantly. Why had I said that? I was angry at his chauvinistic criticism. I hadn't written the chapter as an advertisement for my sexuality as Norman implied. I was trying to show my feelings along the journey from drunk to sober sex, to try to laugh at it and the guilt I felt about my sexuality and its relationship to alcoholism and to drug abuse.

"No, I won't have sex with you," he said. "I'm married to a woman who's jealous. Do you know what a chapter on me would be worth?"

"Your wife should be jealous," I said, putting my hand on his—because this genius didn't understand. The chapter had made Norman nervous, but he had liked it. My anger dissolved when I realized Norman was unable to grasp what I was writing about because he wasn't aware of his own alcoholism. He hadn't taken responsibility for stabbing his ex-wife and the role of alcohol in his violence. His denial of it threw the prurient aspect of my work into relief, thereby dismissing the seriousness of it.

How could I fault him for this? I had been fooled by alcohol too. Then I thought, perhaps I had reached some part of Norman because he had read all twenty-six pages in a noisy, crowded coffee shop without interruption. I also realized that while Norman had been reading about my sexual feelings for Beatty, I had been developing sexual feelings for Norman. And though these feelings excited me, I was disturbed at their presence. I didn't want to be attracted to a man who had had six wives and who-knows-how-many mistresses.

"This Warren piece is good. Just needs editing," Norman said, taking a bite out of his cheeseburger. "Usually when people write, they don't get started until half way in. You know how conversations are—boring, interesting, boring."

Norman seemed hyperactive. His face, flushed. Was it because of my chapter, Warren Beatty, or me? I wondered what was happening at the table.

"What's Beatty like?" Norman asked, finishing his burger.

"He can't be alone. Does grass for sex."

"Does he drink?"

"No, his father was an alcoholic. He has other addictions," I said, putting my napkin on the table. "How do you think he comes off?"

"Good. Great."

Norman grabbed his red ski cap. "I have to go. Study Henry Miller and John O'Hara."

"Wasn't O'Hara a drunk?"

"You an alcoholism counselor?"

"Why O'Hara?"

"He sets a good scene. With economy. Take courses at a university."

"I'm taking creative writing at U.C.L.A."

"Good. Take journalism as well. I'll be in L.A. soon to promote *Tough Guys*. I'll look at what you've done. Try fiction. You can write dialogue."

"Thank you, Norman."

"Never try to breathe life into old writing."

"Isn't that what editing is?"

"No, I'll explain later. I'll have to show you."

"In L.A.?"

"In L.A. One day you'll want to rewrite all five hundred pages and drop that god-awful title. How do you know Picasso loved you, anyway?" Norman laughed.

"It was referring to his son, Claude."

"Still grandiose. I must be going." Norman stood up and helped me with my coat as we walked outside.

I looked up the street at the Lenox Hill Hospital and pointed, "Jerry Hall's giving birth to Mick Jagger's baby as we speak. Over there."

"Glad someone's having children and it isn't me," Norman said. In the daylight he looked older. I could see red veins from drinking. But his looks no longer mattered. Norman's charm was his spirit. A cab pulled up. Suddenly he kissed me on the lips.

"Your lips are wonderful," I said, surprised by his boldness. Yes, I had the choice to push him away. I didn't want to.

"Writers write with their lips," he said. "Yours aren't so bad yourself."

I felt light-headed. We kissed again. And again. Our boots covered in snow. Our faces in sunlight. People passed and stared. He didn't care. Neither did I. So what if he had six wives? He was not capable of fidelity, I told myself. Everyone knew that. He had nine children peppered over six wives. He was the Sultan of Publishing.

"Aren't you glad we didn't have sex?" I asked.

"You bet! You couldn't keep your mouth shut."

"You wouldn't say that in bed."

He kissed me once more. "I'll call you," he said.

And he did—each week for the following nine years.

Chapter 4

When I returned to L.A., I went back to writing with renewed zest. Writing could be lonely. Sometimes frightening. If there was no one to read my work or to hear my thoughts or to guide me, I felt lost and almost blind. But now I had someone to talk to about the written word. Better yet, someone who would listen to me. As far as my acting career was concerned, Ralph Bakshi, who had directed *Fritz the Cat*, just had cast me in his new cinematic cartoon, *Fire and Ice*. Frank Frazetta, the artist who had created Daisy Mae, was going to draw my image from film, or "rotoscope" me. I was playing the Queen of the Fire Planet. Before this, I had been cast as a newscaster in a series for PBS sponsored by the Catholic Church.

But dreams of Norman Mailer haunted me.

Still, I didn't want to spout other people's words. I longed for the quiet times at my typewriter alone with my thoughts. Where I no longer was an object, cartoon or otherwise. Where appearances were just that. Where I said what I believed.

Nevertheless, I had been making a good living as an actress. Comedy was my specialty. I had done two *All in the Family* segments. Carroll O'Connor told me, "You're a good comedian. You have good timing." I played a pregnant woman who, instead of going to an obstetrician, mistakenly went to a veterinarian. On the

Tony Randall Show I played a woman who had been hit by a trolley car and sued the city of San Francisco, claiming the accident had made her promiscuous. She lost the case because the defense proved she was more promiscuous before the trolley car hit her. My character in *Brave New World*, a TV movie, was Morgana Trotsky, the assistant-assistant director of Central Hatcheries (birth control). In *City of Angels* I portrayed a nun with Wayne Rogers as the lead. The director tried to seduce me in my habit. The casting couch was everywhere. For *Man from Atlantis*, I played a mermaid eluding Patrick Duffy. In *Police Story* I was an undercover cop posing as a hooker and almost won a series of my own along with my co-star Ron Leibman.

But my fondest memory of a kindness offered to me by an actress goes to Tuesday Weld. During the filming of *Looking for Mr. Goodbar*, I had to deliver the line, "Sounds like a butch nun." Richard Brooks shouted his direction, "I want a BIG laugh, Carole." I froze. Laughter is the hardest thing for most actors to do. At least it was for me. Tuesday said, "Some direction he gave you. I'll help you out when you come through the door." So as I opened the door, Tuesday Weld tripped on the sofa. I let out a big laugh. She directed *Goodbar*.

It was 1984, and I was forty-two. My looks would be fading. It would be more difficult to get parts as I aged. If I were able to have a career as a writer, I could write at any age. Or had Norman been giving me a line? Was he genuinely interested in helping me with my writing or was he after sex, like so many before him, and therefore willing to say anything? Oh, please, I thought. I was getting ahead of myself. I didn't even know the man. We had just kissed. Period.

Then one night after work I turned on the TV, and there was Norman, handsome and dapper in *Ragtime*. "Men with lipstick on their mouths look like they've just discovered sex," I had read in his novel *Deer Park*. I thought of that now. His lips had been covered with red lipstick after our kiss. Though he was far from just discovering sex, I had the feeling that passion was absent from his life. I felt sad for him, for what I interpreted as his giving up on his sexual appeal.

Feeling over the hill.

Another part of me said, "Don't be gullible."

Norman called me several times. When I proudly told my friends that I had met Norman Mailer, some of them laughed. I didn't understand and ignored whatever criticism came up when I mentioned his name. In Hollywood, the land where no one reads, I discovered the old guard was not impressed by Mailer. Yet when he had walked into Manhattan's celebrity haunt, Elaine's, the Red Sea had parted again. Norman Mailer had East Coast clout. Simple as that.

Soon Norman was calling me every week. He would tell me when he was going to call, and I would arrange my schedule so that I would be by the phone.This was the highlight of my week. I didn't mind if I missed out on the screening of a film or a party. Norman's phone calls inspired me. One call was especially encouraging.

"Hello, kiddo."

"Are you okay?"

"Yeah, I have nine kids for Christ's sake. They keep me sane."

"I mean your health and drinking?"

"Please don't ask me about that," he said, pausing. "Oh, scotch tape your letters. And glue them shut."

"Should I write 'personal'?"

"No, that's too obvious. Judith, my secretary, was hired by Norris and is her good friend."

"I didn't know."

"Now you do. I got those pictures of your mom and you. They were cute."

"Thanks," I said. "I think you'd like Mom."

"I'm sure I would. I'll be in L.A. next week."

"Great! I'll sharpen my pencils."

"Are you writing with number two lead pencil and yellow legal pad like I told you?"

"First draft. Yes."

"Gets you closer to the character. Your feelings."

"What's wrong with number one lead?" I asked

"Number one lead is hard. Tenses up your writing. Makes it brittle."

"Number three?"

"Too soft. Makes writing sloppy. Smudges. Your emotional connection to the lead is diminished by the softness. Are you writing on every line of the memo pad?"

"Sure," I said, staring down at my yellow legal pad.

"Don't do that!"

"Why?"

"Double space your writing. Use the space between the lines for corrections the next time you write."

"Don't you type your work?"

"Good Lord, no. Judith does."

"Wish I had a secretary."

"Maybe one day you will."

"How long do you write at one sitting, Norman?"

"Oh, I take a break each hour. Very important."

"I've done up to four hours in one session."

"Too long. You will tense up. Your brain is a muscle and needs to relax."

"If I'm into it, I just keep going."

"Force yourself to take breaks. You need to write in a relaxed mood."

"Why is that?"

"If you are tense, your writing will be rigid, kiddo. I write when I'm driving my car."

"How can you do that?"

"The voices of the characters sometimes start talking to me."

"Have you ever gotten into an accident?"

"No, but I've gone through a few stop signs in my day."

"How can you concentrate on two things at once?"

"You'll find you'll be doing it too. Sometimes I write while watching TV. Sports are great to watch and write."

"I don't get it."

"I watch the movement, and my mind wanders into whatever I'm writing about until the characters take over my body."

"Sounds supernatural."

"It's a strange feeling, but fun. You'll learn to do it and to like it. I exercise between writing breaks as well. Very important, dearie."

"What do you do?"

"I have a gravity machine."

"What's that?"

"I hang upside down each hour and blood rushes to my head."

"I don't have a gravity machine."

"Lie down. I also have a bed."

"That's a good idea."

"Get your spine flat. It will circulate the blood, which has been used by sitting in an upright position."

"That's a lot to remember, Norman."

"For my anger I have an orgone box."

"What's that?"

"A box like a phone booth sealed off from everyone for sound. I go into it and scream when I'm angry."

"Relieves tension, I bet."

"Sure does. I got it after I stabbed Adele. Now I use it to relieve tension in my writing. Oh, and don't forget to eat."

"Sometimes I do forget, then I grab a yogurt. Fruit. Nuts."

"Bananas are good. Stay away from the candy bars." Norman laughed.

"Why's that?"

"The sugar rush can give you a false sense of euphoria. Make you think that what you are writing is better than it is. All this talk is making me hungry. Listen, I'm staying at the Bel Air."

"Do you like it?"

"Not really. I'll be in a good mood the first day. Then after that I'll turn mean." He laughed. "I'll call you when I get in."

After I hung up, I wondered why Norman had said he would turn mean? He had been considerate since we met. Was Norman warning me about his temper? His Lear-like wrath?

More importantly, what was I getting myself into? Well, we were just friends, I told myself. Nevertheless, whether I was reading Norman's books or looking forward to his weekly calls, I had become obsessed with him. His phone calls gave me hope. He even edited my work over the phone, and he allowed me to tape him. He took risks. That meant he cared about me, I told myself.

Since Norman asked me not to write him because of his wife and his wife's close relationship with his secretary, I began writing him gag letters from fictitious characters. Fans. One was from the top chef and cupcake maker at the Tastykake Factory in Philadelphia. Another was from the head packer of Swanson's Home-style Chicken Dinners, who wanted Norman's autograph. One was from a homosexual cab driver who wanted Norman to autograph a copy of *Ancient Evenings*. Others were from: a preacher, a stripper, a school bus driver, a surfer, a high school principal, an orthodontist, a gynecologist, a nurse, a pro-football player, and a cashier at Walmart.

I read *Ancient Evenings* (enjoyed the sex scenes with Honey Bee), *Barbary Shore* (which I loved), *Why Are We in Vietnam?* (which I hated), *The Executioner's Song* (my favorite), *The Armies of the Night* (refreshing to see that he was able to laugh at himself), *The Fight* (which helped me to respect boxing), *An American Dream,* and whatever Norman Mailer book I could find in hardcover. I had to buy them. It wasn't the same if I went to a library. I wanted to own Mailer. I wanted my own collection.

Chapter 5

Norman called again the following week. He had just checked into the Bel Air Hotel.

"Hello, Carole?" he said with a southern drawl. "It's Norman."

"Did you get my letters?"

"Sure did." He laughed. "How many did you write?"

"About twelve."

"I recognized two. The used-car salesman from Hoboken and the retired Rockette who wanted to give me Samba lessons."

"You didn't pick up on the pizza delivery guy who spilled pizza sauce on *The Naked and the Dead*."

"Not that one too!" Norman laughed. "He wanted me to send him a first edition. Christ! I'll have to go through all my mail. I thought, what a rush of weirdos. You told me you can't write fiction!"

"How long will you be here?" I asked.

"Three days. Would you like to come over? My first interview isn't until two."

"Sure," I said, trying not to sound excited.

"Bring your manuscript. Oh, and don't bother going by the front desk. Come to Bungalow 5."

Ah, so Norman didn't want people to know he was having a female guest. What to wear? I threw on the red knit. It had pleased Sam Peckinpah enough to cast me in *The Killer Elite*. Mailer and Peckinpah had similar sensibilities. Then I grabbed my manuscript, ran out of my apartment, jumped into my yellow Fiat, put the top down, and zoomed off.

I couldn't forget his lips...that strange tingle that went through me when he kissed me on the street corner outside the Lenox Hill Coffee Shop.

It was another sunny, eighty-degree day in southern California as I drove by the bougainvillea on Sunset Boulevard and turned onto Stone Canyon Road. Al Stewart was singing "The Year of the Cat" on the stereo as I pulled into the Bel Air Hotel. The attendant, who looked like a young movie star, parked my car. Only in Hollywood.

Could Norman still get an erection, I wondered as I rushed by the swans in the stream that ran through the lush foliage in front of the Bel Air.

Slow down, I told myself. Don't be too eager. Maybe he doesn't want to have sex with you. This is a choice you could be making for life. Are you sure you want to go through with this? What about your friends. His wife? (Which one? There had been six.) His children? (They were mostly adults. Except for John Buffalo. Why would he have to know? And what was wrong with knowing? His father was a philanderer. Didn't anyone in the family accept this? In the world? Acceptance is love. Norman hadn't been faithful to his wives in the past. Why should he be faithful in the present?) And your reputation, I reminded myself. You could be ruined if you allow him to have sex with you.

I inhaled and calmly knocked on the door while my mind raced with excitement. Thoughts zigzagged across my mind as I composed myself to stand as primly as possible while the door opened. I smiled.

"Well, well, good to see you again, Carole," Norman said formally. He was shorter and plumper than I remembered and wearing khakis and a white shirt. "Come in."

He was old-fashioned. I sat in a corner chair. Terror seized me. Listen. Let him do the talking.

"My, you look different," Norman said, opening a split of champagne. "You were dressed so conservatively in New York."

Wrong outfit. Mailer was a Harvard graduate. Peckinpah wasn't.

"Would you like some champagne?" he asked.

Norman didn't even remember that I was writing about alcoholism.

"No, thank you. I'll have a Diet Coke."

"Oh, that's right. You don't drink. I hope you don't mind if I do." His walk was a waddle.

Speechless, I didn't know what to say. My thoughts had been so bold. Confronted with reality, I became the coward. The room was formal—like Norman. Silent. No music. Dull. My stomach growled.

What should I say? Talk about him, not your manuscript.

"Why are you here, Norman?" I asked.

"To promote *Tough Guys Don't Dance*," he said, handing me the glass of soda. "I'm doing *Johnny Carson* tomorrow night."

"Do you get nervous on talk shows?" I asked, pulling my skirt over my knees.

"Me? No," he said, smiling. "I enjoy it. One day you'll be doing them."

Sure, I thought. He was baiting me. Setting me up.

"You think I'll ever get published?" I asked.

"That chapter on Warren Beatty is terrific. Bring it with you?"

I nodded.

"Let's begin with that. Shall we work at this table where I can do some editing? Why don't you sit here." Norman pulled two chairs side by side and put on his reading glasses. "Show me that chapter."

He had not touched me or kissed me. No crude remarks. No flirtation. He was being the perfect gentleman. Maybe he *was* faithful. He did want to reread that Warren Beatty chapter in which Warren had three orgasms in one night. Maybe he needed to read about sex in order to have it. Some men looked at pictures to get erections. Norman looked at words.

He started to read. Pounding his fist on the table again when he liked something and mumbling my dialogue as he read. He was vicariously enjoying each sentence, each orgasm. With his pen he made some marks.

I felt proud. Grateful. He wanted to help me. He was offering his mind to me. I'd be his Eliza Doolittle if he'd let me, I thought, as I pulled my chair closer and began to relax. I was no longer worried about ruining my life. I was focused on pleasing Norman.

Norman laughed to himself. "You can write a sex scene. A writer writes what a writer knows," he said to the page. He didn't look at me. He preferred my words. I was getting jealous of my work.

I reeked of Shalimar. I'd spent half an hour curling my lashes, putting on eyeliner, eye shadow, blush, lip liner. Gloss. My earrings were from Ylang Ylang.

Their latest collection. Who was he fooling? My looks had gotten attention. Corporations paid to have America look at me. That's what modeling was. Because of my looks I'd picked up Bobby De Niro, Sean Connery, Richard Gere, Peter Sellers, Matt Dillon, Marcello Mastroianni, Warren Beatty, Rod Stewart, Clint Eastwood, and Rip Torn.

Norman read on.

I crossed my legs and thought, *You want to be a writer? Forget you for a minute. Especially what you look like. Boring. Observe. Others. What's behind their eyes, not what's painted on them or their label, wrapper, name!*

For a solid hour Norman read. When he finished the Beatty chapter, he said, "Was Warren Beatty really that good?"

"I wrote it like it was. Isn't that what a writer should do?"

"Precisely." Norman studied me.

"Where's that chapter on Claude Picasso?" I turned to the page and felt Norman's eyes staring at mine. Then he turned back to my work and began to read for another hour. When he finished, he said, "Did you ever meet Pablo?"

"Yes," I said.

"I'd like to see that chapter. Come, let's sit on the sofa. My back's tired."

I followed Norman and sat by his side.

"Well, you have a lot of work to do, but you can do it. You have the experiences. Did you ever think of writing a novel?" Norman asked, placing his arm on the back of the sofa.

"I don't know how to."

"I could teach you."

"Would you? I did try a short story."

"What was it about?"

"A female flasher."

"A female flasher!" Norman laughed. "I'd like to read that."

"Would you?"

"Bring it tomorrow. What time is it?

"Noon."

"I have until two," he said, placing his hand on my shoulder. He pulled me toward him. His face was inches from mine. Awkwardly his lips met mine. He wrote with those lips. Tiny cushions of wisdom. I felt his tenderness. It was a long kiss. My mind stopped racing. Plotting. Rewriting. I relaxed. His lips felt safe. He wasn't going to hurt me. His touch wasn't like that. I didn't have to worry about my reputation. He would protect me. He'd keep it a secret. From all. I'd be his secret. His kiss wasn't aggressive or desperate, like an older man's kiss could be. His lips had confidence. They could feel. We were beginning. I'd stop thinking and let him run the show. After all, he was the genius.

He placed his left hand on my knee and slowly ran it under my skirt, up the inside of my thigh. No words. He kissed me again. Gently he squeezed my flesh, moving upwards. I let him. I was his student. After all. His right hand held my shoulder. His tongue touched. Taunted. His tongue was his mind. He wrote with his tongue. His lips, transmitters of words. His pen, only the instrument. I was kissing his creativity, the real thing. I felt light-headed. Confused.

He pulled away. "We'd be more comfortable in the bedroom." His voice was melodic.

This was it. No getting cold feet now. No running out the service exit now. Mr. Pulitzer Prize, National Book Award Winner, father of nine, husband of six wants to take you to his bedroom. What are you waiting for? I was frightened. His lips made me forget control. *You're a coward*, a voice said. *A phony! I mean, really!* Didn't Norman write, "No fuck was in vain?"

Indecision took a powder. Self-doubt put on hold. I stood up, kicked off my high heels, and started for the bedroom.

"No, no," said Norman. "Wear your shoes."

Norman followed me into the bedroom and began unbuttoning his shirt. Casually he unzipped his fly, took off his pants and shirt and neatly hung them over a wooden hanger in the closet.

I lay on the bed watching the genius strip. Nothing sexy there.

He stood at the edge of the bed, his hands on his hips, his belly protruding. Below, his enormous and thick penis. A boxer's cock. Big, hearty, and ready for the ring. It knew how to move. When to enter. When to exit and what to say. Mailer spoke with his dick. His handshake. His signature. His calling card. It had style. Born and raised on a *Barbary Shore* in Brooklyn.

I lay on the bed mesmerized.

"Come stand beside me. I want to undress you," he said. A command.

I obliged. A master's voice.

Excited by the thought, he said, "No, you stand at the bottom of the bed. I want to direct."

I focused on his mouth, the lips he claimed he wrote with. He was laughing. I stood by the bed both bewildered and excited by the thoughts of Norman's bizarre and marginally sane mind. I mean, he had stabbed a woman. His wife, yet. I looked around the room for sharp objects. Nothing in sight. No knives, razor blades, screwdrivers, dental tools, swords, toothpicks, bottle openers, corkscrews, pistols, or putting irons.

He smelled like the country, an afternoon in the sun. High on a grassy knoll. An I-can-smell-like-I-want-and-you're-not-gonna-make-me-take-a-bath kind of smell. A take-me-as-I-smell-or-get-out-from-under-my-nose kind of scent. His body odor was olfactory pleasure. 100% Boxer Rebellion. One whiff of Norman got me higher than a whiff of gin, rum, tequila, bourbon, scotch, or Ripple.

I stood at the foot of the bed, awaiting General Mailer's instruction.

As he climbed onto the mattress his belly was so big and his legs so thin that he reminded me of Humpty Dumpty. But what did it matter what he looked like? What's looks got to do with it? He pulled at his stomach, slapped it a bit, then yanked. His pride engulfed with thoughts of things to come, pointing toward the ceiling. Nothing half-mast about Norman Mailer. No lighthouse for the blind. He knew why we were in Vietnam. He stood up for what he believed in—sex and human bondage. He had enslaved others, but I was not going to be ruled and ruined by this beautiful specimen of well-crafted sentence structure, syntax, and hyperbole all rolled into one Giant Dick.

"Now, my sweet," he said. "Undo those laces on your bodice. I want to see your many splendors."

I undid the laces.

"Show me your breasts."

I pulled the dress away. My breasts exposed for the literary world.

"My, what perfect pink nipples," Norman said to his model. "Touch them for me."

Oh, God, I thought. How embarrassing. I didn't even know the man. What did he think I was? "Hey, Norm," I wanted to shout, "A woman may be enslaved sexually, yet dominate the man. Remember? *Sexus Miller*. Yes, I'll do what you want, but I'm not going to like it." I hated to touch my own breasts. It made me feel ashamed. I'd been taught sex was a sin. Dirty. Hard to forget that one. Norman had nailed me. On the Rosy Crucifixion. Guilt over my own live body. I could exhibit it. Flaunt it. Talk about it. Write about it. Put it on a poster. You could touch it. But I couldn't touch it. No way. That was bad.

"Miss Mallory, you're not obeying my direction," Mr. Mailer reminded his student.

I touched my breast.

"Circle those delicate nipples with your fingers."

I squeezed my nipples quickly to get it over with and told myself this was a medical exam.

"Miss Mallory, gently. Always gently. How can I teach you sentence structure when you are unwilling to be honest about experiencing the pleasures of your own body?"

What crap! I hoped this wasn't a line from a character in his next novel. Never knew with a writer whose words they were spouting. Theirs or their characters'. I grimaced and followed direction.

"Why that face? Is the thought of having sex with me that repugnant?"

My God! He had confused my feelings for myself with my feelings for him. Narcissists do that.

"Good Lord, no," I said. "Ever since I read *Ancient Evenings* I've wanted to have sex with you." A lie.

"Bet you say that to every Pulitzer Prize winner," he said, laughing.

Why, he was laughing at me! Why not? I was being an ass. I wanted it over. I'd rather be writing.

"Pull your skirt up to your waist."

I lifted my skirt and felt all of three years old. Or like I was modeling again for *Cosmopolitan*.

"What a beauty! Black bikinis suit you, my dear. I'll have to buy you some black lingerie with holes cut out for your nipples."

A lingerie freak. Nothing literary about Frederick's of Hollywood.

"Take off your panties. I want to experience your soul."

I pulled off my G-string and threw it on the bed.

"My, dear, you are a Capricorn."

God, how did he know? "How did you know?"

"I'm the genius, remember? I'll ask the questions, Miss Mallory. Take that god-awful dress off your luscious body and stand there so that I can study your many charms." Norman's voice was musical. I tried to listen to his rhythm rather than his words.

I pulled my dress over my head, threw it on the floor, and kicked off my heels.

"NO! No. Leave them on."

Norman clasped his penis, which had grown. And then some.

"Darling, you are a splendid thing."

I AM NOT A THING! I wanted to shout, but then thought, who am I to change a chauvinist's spots? So I stood there naked in high-heeled sandals for what felt like a decade of *I Love Lucy* reruns.

He continued to fondle his cock and pushed out his lower lip.

Hands by my side I studied his body as he surveyed mine. If his penis weren't so beautiful, I would have left. Maybe I'd turn him into my Henry Higgins. But then he'd have to think I'm subservient. I'd pretend he was Rex Harrison. He would be a new experience. All I had to do was shut my eyes.

On that thought I shut my eyes.

"Are you ill, my dear?" Norman asked without humor.

I opened my eyes and thought of strawberry cheesecake, then gazed seductively at Norman.

"That's better," he said.

I was getting hungry. It was almost lunchtime.

"Now turn around. I want to see all of your treasures."

I turned around.

"Ah, what a cul!"

What's a cul? I wondered.

"That's French for ass, my pet."

He was reading my mind. Had he even invaded my thoughts? Couldn't I have some privacy?

"You'll make a good student, my darling. Now bend over and show me your secret!"

I bent over with pleasure, one asshole to another.

"Dear, dear, you are lovely."

Five minutes seemed to lapse, during which I thought about the vacuuming I had to do, the dishes in the sink, the cats that had to be fed. That script to read for Monday. The dinner party to get ready for at Morton's, that manicure at three o'clock at the Beverly Hills Hotel. And that copy of *The Ginger Man* I had to return to Laurel Delp.

"What a spirit you have, my dear!"

What the hell did spirit have to do with assholes? A backhanded compliment, no doubt. Gotta watch writers. Never listen to them.

"I'm getting dizzy," I said, yawning.

"Yes, my pet, come into my arms. It feels good to be wanted," Norman said sincerely.

"Kiss me, Norman," I said.

He did, and that tingling began. He held me tight, and I felt his taut flesh. Though he had a belly, his body was firm. No cellulite.

Not bad for sixty-one, I thought, enjoying his cuddle. I felt safe again. All the talk was play acting. Maybe he was insecure under all that macho, old-fashioned dialogue.

I mean maybe he felt he had to say that stuff because he thought I wanted to hear it. Maybe he was trying to please me. Maybe he wanted me to like him. Maybe Norman Mailer cared what I thought. About him. I liked that thought. Maybe I had been unfair to judge him so quickly. I ran my fingers through his white curls and played with the white hairs on his chest. I liked them. Long and curly like a fluffy pillow. I wanted to lie on his curlicues and dream. Think nice thoughts. Could he be kind or would he be cruel? He had always been considerate to me. So what if his dialogue had been old-fashioned? How the hell must he have felt when this sort of young twit showed up and threw a chapter about a one-night stand with Warren Beatty in his face, wearing a tight red knit, fuck-me-sandals, and three-inch dangling earrings from Ylang Ylang? I mean, really. Who did I think I was to laugh at him?

He was the great writer, and he had spent two hours reading my dreck.

Get serious, I thought, running my tongue around his nipple. He liked that. He liked to be given pleasure. He moaned. He craved attention. Sexual attention. Was he gettin' any? I wondered. I felt years of orgasms bottled up in his scrotum. A sexual pressure cooker about to explode. I would make him feel better, I thought as I felt him nibbling my curlicues as he mumbled, chewed, licked, cajoled, sweet-talked, caressed, entertained, interviewed, and enjoyed me.

I sighed. Eyes closed, I wasn't thinking of Rex Harrison. No, I was thinking of Norman Mailer between my legs. Between my ears. Norman Mailer, the tough guy.

Norman Mailer wasn't so tough. He was vulnerable and didn't want anyone to know it. That's why the roar. That's why the do-ray-ME-braggadocio. My, how his lips knew their way around my world. They no longer talked. I was able to feel. I forgot about all those dirty girls in me saying I was naughty, bad, WRONG, trying to turn me into the "tough girl." Why, I wasn't the tough cookie at all. I'd just crumbled too many times to let Norman or anyone know the hurt, the rejection. Maybe he was hiding his hurt from me. Maybe that's why he talked like that. Saying what he thought I wanted to hear. Everyone gets afraid when the sheets are down.

Oh, his lips felt good. I sighed again. I thought of nothing. A void. I felt free. Loose. Young. Norman Mailer's lips were making me feel young. Who the hell had I been kidding? I was forty-two. No spring poulet. And I was laughing at Norman's age. He was making me feel like a kid again. Like a goddamn born-again. I liked that. I liked to pretend that he was Daddy Norman. I relaxed some more and had an American dream as Daddy Norman rub-a-dub-dubbed my cruise ship, my vessel, my masthead, my deer's park, my oar and rudder, jib and then some, my surgeon general, too, my main attraction. That was what it was, and I was loving it.

I felt good, happy. No more laughing at him, no more ridiculing him. No more nasties. Out! OUT spots of wicked deprecation. Out of my wonderful fucked up, forever frightened, tortured soul. I said, I felt, I screamed.

I yanked at his white hair. He slapped my thigh. I screamed. It was over, and I was his, and that's how it happened.

He turned down the light; the voices in my head quieted, and he held me close. "You seemed to like that, my sweet," said Norman, no longer the wicked. I was in his arms once more, except now I wanted to be here. There. Everywhere with him. I liked his flesh. FLASH. I liked his FAT.

"Watch out!" a voice said. "Don't get too comfortable. He's a married man."

"Everybody's got problems," another voice said.

I blanked out on that one.

"Tomorrow's another day," a child sang into my left ear.

I put cotton in the right ear and identified with Scarlet.

"Did you like that, my lovely?" he asked.

"Norman, is this what editing feels like?" I asked.

He laughed. He always laughed at my sillies. He liked to laugh. He needed to laugh. I wondered whether inside there was such sadness. Nope. Didn't want to know too much about that. Rescue missions, my specialty. That's when the pain's the greatest.

"Stay on the surface," a voice said. "Enjoy the sex. You haven't had any for a while. Who are you trying to kid?"

"Yep, editing is like this," he said, squeezing me in his arms.

I nuzzled my head under his armpit. Lots of hair there to pile upon. He smelled good—wet and dewy and good.

He squeezed my arms, my buttocks, my breasts. His hands were tiny wandering minds. Exploring, searching. For what? I didn't know. Experience. That was it. Norman Mailer was in love with experience.

So was I.

"Now, Norman, it's my turn," I said, pushing him gently down on the bed. My, it was fun to push Norman Mailer around. Don't often get a chance to tell a genius what to do when you're a Hollywood starlet on the run from the tinsel hanging all over town.

"Ah, my pet, tell me what to do. Please, I'm your patient."

"Lie back."

"Yes, nurse."

"Spread your legs," I said, shocked at my assertiveness.

Norman looked down at me a bit perplexed. Though he would relinquish control, there were riders, conditions, negotiations always to be made.

"I like to watch," he said.

"Lie back. Enjoy. Be quiet," I said.

I began with Mr. Genius and Lust. Terror seized me. Could I do it? Would he find me out? I was a fraud on this turf. On his turf. He had had so many women. So many loves who knew their way around this part of him that I loved but was hopeless at making love to. I would try.

Not tell him my fears. Think positively like a good Girl Scout about to give her first blowjob to the scoutmaster in the bushes. The more men I had, the worse I felt. If I would just stop thinking about me and think about him.

It was that old ex-husband who did it to me. Told me I was lousy at it as I would go up and down, and he'd push my head onto his. I'd gag. Then do it again. I felt nothing. Anger. Rage. Fear. Inadequacy. But Norman wasn't my ex. Norman wanted my lips. Wanted me. To be. To do it my way. And that was nice. He didn't tell me how, or where. Nope. I told him. That's right, I told him. "Lie back and enjoy," and I would give him pleasure and erase that stuff from the past. Haunt me no more. Don't compare. Do. Enjoy. Be. I was accepting his and forgetting me.

He moaned. No direction. No "My wife does it better." No "My six wives did it better." He was silent.

I looked up at his face. Eyes closed. Good. Control over. He was letting me lead. Trust beginning. Doing it my way, not Sinatra's, who liked to run the show too.

Oh, stop your inner monologue. He'll lose interest because of your self-absorption. Concentrate. Give pleasure. Think of him. Love him. This minute. Second. Molecule. Moment. His tenderness bolted out of him. His knees jerked. Kicked! He groaned. Thank God he didn't announce his coming.

I caressed him while he returned to his infantile self. Mr. Giant Phallus had retired. Testosterone at bay. Round two. Over.

I scooted up from between his knees to between his arms and said, "Hold me."

He did.

"Thank you," he said.

"You're welcome," I said.

Seconds later he was snoring, and we hadn't yet done it.

There was time. *Plenty*-of-time. He was sixty-one. I was forty-two. He had twenty years of knowledge on me. Wisdom.

Watch it, a voice said.

SHUT UP, I told her, and soon I was sleeping too. I dreamed about getting published and being Norman Mailer's mistress. I would make him my mentor, and he'd make me his muse. That could be feasible. Nothing else was in the cards. A hangman's deck. I looked the other way.

After about an hour, I felt him mount me. On top of me. Straddling me. Going at me. Where had all this vigorous interest manifested itself? I was unprepared. Always the unexpected with Norman. Yep, he was out to snooker me. Along with the rest. Spin my head around and then some. A pineapple upside-down cake I'd be when he got through with me. Two nuts and a fruitcake. All marbles lost.

His hands were by my shoulders. His body above mine. His movements, vigorous. Pounding. Pounding. His face above mine. His Paul Newman blues. His lips protruding.

"Come to the edge of the bed, my dear," he said.

I did.

He moved better standing or straddling sideways like a big bear holding his cub or like a papa kangaroo, and I would be tucked in his pouch.

"Hold me. Think warm. Release. Do you feel me? I'm kissing you. With my lips. Squeezing you, holding you. So there. No! I don't want you to come yet. You have so many faces. The vixen. The smile of the vixen. Hold my cock. Feel its warmth!"

He was like that. This. The above. And then some. Yes, he was as he did, did, did. Back and forth, up and down, round and round we went. I watched. He performed. I liked it that way.

Too much, a voice said.

So what! I said.

You're going to get hurt, she'd say.

Shut up! I'd say.

I closed my eyes and began to love. To let myself love. No strings. No clauses of ifs, ands, or buts. No oops! What will the neighbors think? I wasn't in love with the neighbors. I was in love with Norman Mailer. Yep, I sure was. And that felt mighty good.

We napped again. He held me and snored again. I felt like a baby in his arms. And that was okay. When he got up, he put on a white terry cloth robe and tied it like a boxer would around his waist. With his white hair, white robe, slim calves, light blue eyes, he suddenly was handsome. (I liked to think the two orgasms helped too.) He had no age. As I watched him put on the robe, I realized he wasn't fat. God had just forgotten to give him a waist. His chest and tummy had merged without thinking. God gave him brains instead of a waist. And that's the truth. His body was firm and tight, and he was in shape.

"Swimming," he said. "Climbing stairs," he said.

Fucking, I'd say. I was convinced he had mistresses all over town, America, and *le monde entier*.

"Carole, at my age," he would say, "it's difficult to get an erection."

But he never had that problem with me. Not once. Not in nine years.

Pops went up. Sure did. He'd look at me naked in one of those not so trashy lingerie getups…G-strings, corsets, teddies, suspenders and nothing else, body paint, ribbons, Band-aids, cellophane, rubber bands, rubber cement, string. Once I wrapped myself up like his naked gift—ribbons, bows, and all. For his birthday.

Each week I'd surprise him with a new outfit.

Each week he'd want to play a new game…doctor, manicurist, masseur, Hollywood director (that was a favorite), garage mechanic, chief, cook, and bottle washer.

Each week Norman would knock on my bedroom door.

"Who's there?" I'd say.

"Herr Lipschitz," his character of the week might say. Or Ernie the gardener. Or Charles the masseur. And so on. Then, of course, there was always the possibility of my being on top. I liked that. He did too. Took one year to get there. Be Top Dog. Top Gun. Get a view from his bridge. He never complained.

Except for that time he asked me to tie him up. To a chair. Kicked me that time, he did. Bad, Mailer, bad. Down, Mailer, down.

Norman led me each week. First I'd dress up, then undress according to direction. He just stared at me and smiled, studying and yanking the brain between his legs.

Now his penetration was more rigorous. His pounding, more vigorous. I could feel him growing. Inside of me. His already big self was getting bigger. Inside of me. He was being born. Inside of me.

Chapter 6

When I was thirteen, my father had an operation that left him mentally incapacitated and physically deformed. In an attempt to make him smile, I began to call him "my favorite Daddy." That was my way of saying his deformity didn't repulse me as it did others. I wanted him to believe, although it was untrue, that I preferred "Daddy" after surgery.

We had been a team, Herbert E. Wagner and I (Emile was his middle name). Before the operation he was tall, over six feet. He had a big nose with a bump on it like an Indian chief's and blue eyes. The kind that sparkled when he laughed. They especially sparkled when I tried to tell a joke. My father loved laughter, even after the operation.

On Saturdays we'd visit Kresge's five-and-dime at 69th Street in suburban Philadelphia. A big treat for my sister and me. When my mother wouldn't buy me a toy over twenty-five cents, my father would slip me the extra coins and whisper, "Don't tell your mother." Problem was, my father's whisper would be like a foghorn, and my mother would sometimes catch us and bawl us out. But my father would give me the money the next Saturday.

I was especially fond of the times my father wrote at his desk and balanced his general ledger. I was never allowed to touch anything on the desk, let alone open its drawers. Though I did sneak peeks when he wasn't looking. (Maybe this was part of the reason I loved writing.)

Sprawled on the floor by his side, I would cut out dresses for my paper dolls or study the peek-a-boo outfits in my comic books about the heroine Katy Keene, the Pin-Up Queen. She was sexy. I had ostrich legs like my father, which earned me the nickname Toothpick and ridicule from the boys. I would climb many a tree while running from the jeers and catcalls of the guys who made fun of my skinny legs.

My father, a proud graduate of the University of Pennsylvania's Wharton School, worked as an accountant at the Philadelphia National Bank. The bank's president said my father was "a man who never made a mistake." Nights, my father worked at Westinghouse, and on weekends he sold insurance and read. *Think and Grow Rich* by Napoleon Hill was his favorite book. My father's idol was his great uncle General Lou Wagner, who led the Battle of Bull Run and became a Civil War hero. My father was blue-blooded and proud of it.

Lifestyles of the Rich and Famous would later be my mother's favorite television program. *The Grapes of Wrath* could have been her biography. Years later, when I took her to see the play on Broadway, she didn't like it. "Why?" I asked her. "Because that's just how it was," she replied. Born in 1900 on a farm in Shoemakersville, Pennsylvania, my mother was the eldest of twelve children. Her father was an alcoholic. In a drunken rage he once poured a basin of boiling water on my wheelchair-bound grandmother.

Norman Mailer thought *Death of a Salesman* told the story of both our fathers.

My father wasn't home much because he worked so hard. When he was home, I was by his side. When he returned from the bank at 5:00 p.m. sharp, I would be waiting by the door, listening for his honk as he drove his Chevy (he owned only Chevys) into the driveway. I would be dressed up for him. An hour later he was out the door, and I wouldn't see him until the next evening. Five hours a week I saw my father, not including weekends.

The winter of 1985 (and for six winters to come), I would see Norman approximately five hours a week. Before he arrived, and before we made love, I would dress up for him. He loved to look at me, and I loved to please him.

The remainder of the week I would write, and the following week he would edit my writing. Like my father, Norman worked hard. His diligence inspired. He would stress the importance of his time in relation to his writing and the money he would earn from his work. He wanted me to be aware of this with my writing.

"Bill Styron can afford seven years writing a novel," Norman would say. "I can't."

My father would also impress upon me the economy of time.

My father's breakdown began in 1953 when I was in seventh grade. He developed a nervous twitch and was unable to answer the phone. He had to quit all three jobs, though he still sold insurance to the church (which cancelled their policy after my father's operation). The doctors didn't know what was wrong with him. Mother, who had been a nurse, took my father to doctor after doctor.

After the breakdown, eating was humiliating for my father. His eyes would blink, his nose would run, his gums and eye teeth would be exposed. He would be forced to make grotesque expressions with his mouth each time he would twitch. Food would fly from his fork to a wall or to the floor. My father would have difficulty chewing and keeping his food in his mouth.

When we were in a restaurant, my mother would say, "Why do you make faces like that, Herb? People are staring at us."

My mother wouldn't understand.

When people would stare at my father, I would stare back at them. "Take a picture. It'll last longer!" I'd shout. Then they'd stop; they'd stare at me instead.

At home, I remember wanting to eat as fast as possible. Getting away from the dining table would calm my nervousness. Watching my father eat became torture for us all.

Protecting my father after his nervous breakdown became my role. I became his caretaker. Twelve at the time of his breakdown, I learned that if I put on makeup and made myself as pretty as possible, people would stare at me instead of my father, and he would suffer less. In public, he twitched, accompanied with grunts and groans. Sometimes he would accidentally bump into people. Some were kind; others leered, whispered, pointed, laughed, and ridiculed—as though my father were a circus performer. A freak. "Let's get your sideshow on the road," I said to him as he twitched away like a giant metronome. He would smile. "We're going to Howard Johnson's."

In those summers, when I worked at Howard Johnson's, it became his favorite restaurant. Though it was just across the street. The "street" was Route 1, a four-lane highway, so my father would have to be driven. Walking through traffic would have been impossible. The hostesses at the restaurant were not always kind.

"Has Daddy gone off to see his girlfriend?" my mother would ask when my father disappeared, which happened often. We never knew what he would do or where he would go.

We would always be afraid. "What will Daddy do next?" my mother would say.

But going to Howard Johnson's for a Sunday dinner was a real treat for my father.

"Sit in the car until I get us a table," I told my family. Then, wearing my best dress and prettiest makeup, I waited in line for a table. Sometimes I felt like a spy or a model. I enjoyed being in disguise. I was hiding the secret of my father's deformity from the hostess and the patrons of this fine establishment. My father would want a booth. One by the window. Or in a corner where he would be less noticed.

If I were alone when I walked into Howard Johnson's, the hostess would give me a good table, then I'd throw my coat in the booth and run out to get my family. If the hostess saw my father before she gave us a table, she seated us in the back of the restaurant near the swinging kitchen doors with the accompanying odors and noises. My father didn't like this table and felt bad if we had to sit there, feeling ugly and unwanted. An inferior table made him feel the same. I wondered if my father suffered more because of his condition and the botched operation or because he had been ostracized in a world of which he no longer felt a part.

Telling my father to wait in the car until I got a table was a trick I learned to protect my father. At an early age I questioned the importance of appearances, but at the same time I learned to use my looks to get what I wanted. Though modeling would teach me what others considered beautiful, I would never feel beautiful. Except when I drank. My beauty had been a weapon to protect my father from pain. Some part of his pain would become a part of me. Alcohol, drugs, and sex would help me to forget. For a short time.

In 1954, one of my father's doctors suggested spending some time in a warm climate might help him. So my mother took my father and me to Florida while my sister stayed in suburban Philadelphia because she was in high school.

In Bradenton, my father's condition worsened.

A neighbor said to mother, "The boys in the Korean War were helped by shock treatments. Maybe they would help Herb."

My mother, who was always looking for a solution, arranged for shock treatments. "Won't someone get me out of my misery?" my father would shout. My mother tried. After each shock treatment my father would run around our house like an animal on fire. "I'm not a radio, for Christ's sake," he would shout. "Running electricity through my head doesn't make sense." My father never wanted the treatments, but my mother insisted on seven.

It was the time I was discovering boys. It was the time Nat King Cole sang, "It's Cherry Pink and Apple Blossom White." It was the time I fell in love with Tommy, my first true love. Mother said he was from the wrong side of the tracks. That's why I liked him. He was real. We had a tree house outside my grandmother's house in Bradenton. When my father was given his shock treatments, Tommy and I would be making out in the jungle nearby or in the tree house or walking the railroad tracks with his machete looking for snakes or reading comic books under the palm trees. (My grades went from As in suburban Philadelphia to Cs and Ds in Florida.)

When my father would come home after his shock treatment, I would teach him to speak as he was unable to. I remember eating my Rice Krispies each morning and teaching my father to talk. In a few hours he would be able to speak again. But by then I would be at school. I took the bus. Blacks had to sit in the back. With my black friends, I went to the back of the bus too. I didn't want to sit with whites who thought like that, and I didn't like hostesses in restaurants who treated my father as though his deformity made him inferior. A twitching father who was like a giant metronome, I told myself, was better than no father at all.

Then my father's twitching grew worse. Nothing seemed to help him.

After three months of Florida sun and no improvement in my father, we returned home. There were new doctors. One suggested an experimental operation. Mother didn't want it. My father, who now had been given shock treatments against his wishes, wanted it. "Anything to get me out of my misery," he said.

So the doctors gave my father a lobotomy. I was in ninth grade and cheerleading in a pep rally.

During the operation, the doctors discovered my father had been suffering from Parkinson's disease and apologized for their misdiagnosis. The lobotomy aggravated the Parkinson's. It had been a mistake. Still the doctors sent my mother a bill. "Let those butchers try to collect," my mother said.

Though the operation left my father mentally incapacitated, he still laughed at my jokes, only now with just a grin. He was no longer able to blink. He had a fraction of his senses. He was emotionally unavailable. When I recovered from the shock of what had been done to him, I became grateful for the portion of him not destroyed by the surgeons. A portion of the man I loved was better than none of him.

Then the doctors suggested my father be put in an asylum to separate him from my sister and me. My sister was four years older. While my father was in the mental hospital, he helped the nurses make beds and wove baskets for me. "Your father doesn't belong here," a nurse said. The doctors had been afraid of the effect he would have on my sister and me.

When he came home, I was happy.

Always looking for a new solution, the doctors put my father on a medicine called L-dopa besides the Thorazine and Miltown he had been taking. L-dopa, among its other properties, was a sexual stimulant. I remember my mother rejecting my father's sexual advances. "Ach, Herb, no! Get away from me," she would say. "He can't keep an erection," she later told me. "His twitching makes it impossible for him to have sex."

Mother would find pages of what she called "dirty books" under his mattress. "Herb, why are you reading this filth?" she would say and then hit him as he twitched away.

"Daddy, you can hide it under my mattress," I said to him behind her back.

Mother, though she was now head nurse at the Jefferson Hospital in Philadelphia, didn't understand and later confessed that she had been taking his medicine too. She had been raised strict Pennsylvania Dutch and had been taught that sex was a sin. Her family had painted hex signs on their barns to protect them from the evil spirits.

There were times the police, who were wonderful, would find my father in his Black Watch plaid bathrobe trying to cross the highway or driving our car to the corner mailbox. When he drove, he was "straight as a stick," he used to say. The police brought my father home. We had to hide the car keys from him.

Sometimes I felt that my father was like a pet. If only I could have had a leash for him then I would know he was safe.

Going to 69th Street's "dirty movies" was another one of his escapes. He would disappear from the house and, in his Black Watch plaid bathrobe and slippers, take the bus into Philadelphia.

Afraid for his safety, I bought locks for all the doors and locked the house from the inside so that he could not get out. Then I hid the keys.

One day my sister, my mother, and I heard screams from the upstairs bathroom. My father began having seizures from all the medication. He had developed epilepsy. While my sister was driving through the congested traffic in the heart of Philadelphia, my father, who was seated next to her, had a convulsion. She shoved her fingers in his mouth, and he almost bit them off.

Every night my father's mattress would squeak throughout the house from his thrashing. He could not go to sleep until the medication knocked him out. My sister, my mother, and I all had trouble sleeping. Mother would give me

Phenobarbital some nights to sleep. Later I would develop an addiction to sleeping pills.

In time I became attracted to unavailable men.

No, Norman would not divorce; nevertheless, I was grateful that he gave a part of his life to me and that I had a portion of his love. If five hours a week were all he could afford to share with me, I would cherish those hours. I would accept them as being all the time a man who had six wives, nine children, an agent, a lawyer, a secretary, several publishers, and grandchildren was physically able to share with me. Norman Mailer had a hectic, dramatic, and chaotic lifestyle that he thrived on. I felt respect for him. I was especially grateful that he was healthy. Reasonably healthy.

Though Norman wouldn't be able to make us a family, he had the mind that my father had had taken away. Norman could share his genius with me. Norman and I became a sort of family. A team. Not a wife and a husband, but a writer and an editor. Or so he made me feel.

Any shame I may have felt for having an affair with a married man was sanitized, dispelled, and made wholesome when Norman began to assume the identity of my father.

Norman's guilt was also assuaged. When he assumed my father's name, he became a father figure, but from his perspective or subconscious it could have been his own father's image he was imitating, that of a philanderer. In our affair Norman and I were reliving our conflicted childhoods.

Several times before Norman walked into my apartment, I would overhear him talking to himself as though he were rehearsing dialogue as he paced up and down the hallway. Was he trying to decide what to say? Was he trying to shed feelings he had brought from his home? Was he trying to organize his lies and lives? Was he creating a new character from a novel he was about to write? Was he telling his wife a fictionalized account of our relationship? Was he pretending to be talking to his agent? His publisher?

In 1988 at a PEN benefit, where I was wearing a white silk cowl neck gown and with my hair brushed off my forehead, cropped short, I was introduced to *Vanity Fair* editor-in-chief Tina Brown and her husband, Random House publisher Harold Evans. Both were serious publishers of Mailer. They stared at me, speechless. I felt like a ghost as they looked at me, then through me. I felt like I could have written *War and Peace*. Harold Evans began to spout compliments. Tina Brown remained silent as we observed each other. I wondered what Norman had told this omnipotent couple?

And though Norman made me feel like we were on the same team, like my father had always made me feel, I had moments of suspecting that behind my back he was sabotaging me and my writing. But because of the help and support he gave me with my writing while we were together, I trusted him.

Tina Brown and Harold Evans could have been judging me for having a relationship with a married man, I thought, even though they had fallen in love when Harold Evans was married to another woman. Most likely they had learned of my sexual relationship with Norman from Norman.

Norman may have reminded me of my father when we were in love, but when our relationship ended, I realized that, unlike my father, Norman had never been on my team and had been slandering my writing and me behind my back.

Chapter 7

When I walked into the bathroom that afternoon in June of 1984 at the Bel Air Hotel and looked in the mirror, I wondered what I was getting myself into. What heartache would follow? How could I survive a relationship with a married man and assume the role of the other woman? Would I be willing to give up part of my identity to be with The Great One?

No, I would have to bolster myself for having to watch Norris Church Mailer on the arm of the man I would grow to love.

In 1989, this would be particularly painful. At a reading, Norman was escorting Norris, who wore a stunning floor-length red fox coat. I looked down at my black cloth coat. He clutched her by her elbow. As I passed them, I said, "Hello, Norman." He turned his head and looked away as if he didn't know me. We had been what I had considered to be in love for six years, and he couldn't acknowledge me. I shouted, "Don't ever call me again." Then I stumbled to my seat and cried. This was the man who used to ask me to bathe him. This was the man who had discussed marriage and its impossibility. This was the man for whom I had given up having a child. I could have gotten pregnant like Norris Church and the wife before her and forced him to marry me, but I wouldn't do that to him. Or to the child.

A tear fell on the frayed cuff of my black blazer. I was frayed, flawed like my jacket. Why was I always choosing men who were half there for me? Men I felt I had to rescue. Men I felt I had to make feel better and subjugate myself in the process. I knew the answer. The doctors had taken so much away from my father that he, too, had only been half there for me.

I blew my nose in a Kleenex and wondered—would I remain childless for the rest of my life?

Oh, I had always told myself that I didn't want children, but I know this was false pride. The truth was that I felt inadequate. Just like I felt tonight. Less than. I just knew I wouldn't be a good mother. I would let my child down.

But I had my writing. Norman had given me one thing. Maybe not a baby, but his wisdom. This was a great gift. He was a confused genius. Maybe time would sort out his cruelty.

As I was leaving the Bel Air in the summer of 1984, Norman asked, "Are you free for dinner tonight?"

"Sure," I said, suddenly forgetting my manicure, my dinner at Morton's, and returning *The Ginger Man* to Laurel Delp.

"Where would you like to dine?" he asked.

"72 Market is new. In Venice."

"Fine. 72 Market it will be."

I wanted to impress Norman by introducing him to Dudley Moore, a friend, who owned the restaurant. Dudley would not make us wait.

At 72 Market Street, the maitre d' greeted us, then said, "Please wait by the bar. I'll give you the first table." Dudley was obviously out of town.

After some time, Norman, who was sitting in a green and beige cane chair, smaller than him, began to fidget. "Tom Thumb might feel comfortable here."

"Brasserie Lipp in Paris has the same chairs," I said.

"I don't care if Queen Elizabeth has the same chairs in Buckingham Palace. My ass is going to land in someone's soup in Venice, and I don't mean Italy."

We retreated to my Fiat, threw the top down, and drove off to Morton's, which Norman kept calling Morgan's. At sixty-one, Norman's hearing and memory were beginning to fail.

I knew Peter Morton, another friend, would not make us wait. Getting a good table without a reservation would impress Norman.

Peter Morton greeted us, then said, "Please wait by the bar. I'll give you the first table."

Why would Peter do this when I was in the company of Norman Mailer, whose writing put most of these Hollywood hacks to shame? When I put on my glasses, I realized the restaurant was filled with celebrities. I smiled to a director whom I knew. He reciprocated a curious greeting.

True to Peter Morton's word, when the first table became available, he seated us.

Norman cleared his throat. "Folks in Hollywood aren't going to like what you're doing."

"Isn't that true of all writers? You?"

"I'm not an actor, my dear. Nor do I live in this town."

"I'd love to move back to New York."

Norman frowned and studied his menu.

Why the frown, I wondered?

"Do you mind if I eat garlic?" he asked.

"No."

"Are you going to?"

"No."

"Then I won't. I'll have Chateaubriand. Have whatever you'd like. I'm on an expense account." Norman laid his menu on the table and moved the candle to one side.

"I'll have the veal chop," I said.

"Norris tried to write once. She even had two articles published. Then she quit."

"Goodness, why? Weren't you teaching her?"

"She wasn't able to tell all sides of the situation. A writer has to be brutally honest and tell it all, all around the bend."

"Do I do that?"

"You try. You did in that Beatty chapter. Sometimes good writing can hurt. Takes courage."

"Is my work honest?"

"From what I've seen it succeeds when you laugh at yourself. I love that part of you that laughs when you make a mistake or when I tell you you're being a schmuck. That's a great quality."

"There's a lot of material there."

"Stay in character in your writing. That's very important. I want to see you grow."

"Norman, I can't edit."

"You must learn. Only you can edit your work. Time helps here."

I groaned.

"You have a keen observant eye. Your choice of detail is excellent. That part where you tell the reader that a character did not want people stepping on their white carpet with their shoes on because they were trying to sell the house was terrific."

"That was true. George Hamilton told his guests once at a party not to walk on his carpet. He was into real estate when he wasn't acting."

"Doesn't matter who said it. Like I said, when you write a novel, you're using real life, but changing names. The information is what is important. You use too many details. Selection is the key."

"I think I have trouble with description."

"Watch adjectives here. They're roadblocks. When I met Rosalynn Carter at a party, she told me she was writing a book. I told her to go through her book and take out all of the adjectives."

"Did she do it?"

"The next time I saw her she said, 'Norman, I did as you suggested and my editor said I had a better book because of it. Better than Jimmy's.'"

"You're very sweet. I wanted to tell you I found an author because of you."

"Who's that?" Norman said, sipping his Perrier.

"I want you to guess. It's one of the ones I told you about. I like his clarity, gentleness, tenderness, insight, set-up of scenes, his conciseness."

"Who? Who are you talking about?" Norman asked excitedly.

"Can't you guess from that?"

"No, who?"

"Forster."

"E.M. Forster? Oh, that's so long ago."

"Wasn't that a pretty accurate observation?"

"Yes, pretty good. I'll tell you something funny. You won't believe this. I said E.M. Forster to myself at one point. Read Joan Didion. You'd like *Play It as It Lays*."

"I auditioned for the film."

"I'm talking about writing, Carole. Stay focused. Joan Didion is a great writer."

"Yes, boss."

"Did you read *The Two Mrs. Grenvilles*? Nick Dunne's book," Norman said.

"I have it at home."

"Read it. It's very good."

"It's not bad writing? My friend Chester said it's poorly written. Chester was Nick Dunne's decorator."

"It's good writing. Chester's full of shit. Friends are your worst critics! It's not great writing. But it's very good writing. It's simple, clean, and filled with wonderful detail. Wonderful dialogue."

"When did you read it?"

"I'm reading it now." Norman always had a book on him when he visited me. "I'm enjoying it."

"I have it at home. I started it."

"It's very skillful. It's not a great book, but it's a damn good little book."

"Don't you like my reading Forster?"

"Yes, I do."

"He'd be a great teacher, no?"

"Yeah, you can learn a lot from him."

"I look for someone to do what Chandler did for me, and oddly enough I find him a lot like Chandler. Is that possible?"

"Forster? They both write very simply with telling detail. Their details work for them. They never put a detail in there just to have it in there. Where's our waiter?"

"He'll be here any minute. They're busy, Norman."

Norman looked around the restaurant and nodded to a friend.

I continued. "Maybe that's why I like Forster and Chandler. Do you think my eye is seeing their economy?"

"Yeah, you're probably getting an eye for details from them."

"Do you think I'm good with details?"

"Yeah. Now, we began the conversation with this. Don't make me repeat myself. You put in too many, but your details are one of your assets. You see a lot, and you put it in. Stop looking for compliments."

The waiter appeared. We ordered then resumed our conversation.

"Do you write best if you write slowly?" I asked.

"There are no rules, love. No rules. Sometimes I write best when I'm going very quickly. You can't even tell by how you're feeling."

"That doesn't seem right."

"Sometimes I feel I've done a terrific piece of writing, and it really isn't that good. I was just excited when I was writing it."

"I get very excited when I write."

"And there are times I feel I really didn't do anything very good, and two months, three months later, looking it over, I think, 'Gee, that was so much better than I thought it was. Why didn't I realize that at the time?' So there are no rules."

"When I write a novel, can I put it in the present tense?"

"You can do it. It changes things. There's got to be a reason for being in the present tense. My dear, it's a stylistic mannerism. You can try it. If it sounds better to you, do it that way."

"For some reason it seems to come naturally when I think about it."

"Well, the whole book could be in the present tense. That could work. There are books like that. It makes it very immediate. On the other hand there's no chance to relax for the writer."

"What about the reader?"

"Well, for the reader too."

"Does it make for more tension and drama?"

"It makes more tension, but on the other hand it makes it a little harder to read, I think, 'cause people aren't used to it. So you could do it if you want to. You know, as I said before, there are no rules. There's no rule stronger than doing what you seem to be doing."

"Will you look at my new writing, Norman?"

"If we have a little time, I can go over what you're doing. I'll be able to tell you a little more. Look, you're working well, aren't you?"

"I think so. I find if I take time in the morning, my brain's good. Not tired. I've been going to cafes, restaurants, and writing it. If I don't hurry, the details are richer. I find when I hurry and want to get them out..."

"No, don't hurry. You want to build care in your writing, and concern. Don't start getting slapdash. By the way, what are you reading?" Norman asked.

"I want to read *Presumed Innocent*."

"Oh, Turow's book. You can read it. You'll enjoy it."

"Have you read it?"

"Yeah, it's pretty good. It's not literature, but it's very well done."

"I'm not writing literature, am I?"

"No, but you've got your own flair. You've got something very special. You know you're not like other writers."

"Norman, I brought that novel I'm working on. It's in the car. Could I leave it with you until tomorrow?"

"Sure, I'll do my best to look at it in the morning."

"Tell me some more writers to study."

"Steinbeck."

"*Travels with Charley*?"

"My impression is *Grapes of Wrath* is his best book. Read an author's best book, and then if you really love it, you can go looking into his other books. *Grapes of Wrath* is twice as good as Steinbeck's other books, but I've never read *Travels with Charley*."

The waiter brought our appetizers, and after a quick dinner, we returned to the Bel Air where Norman fell asleep in my arms.

Feeling that I was giving too much of myself to Norman and afraid of the intimacy that sleeping with him would create, about midnight I returned to the comfort and privacy of my own bed in my own apartment. I wanted to be alone and for this night was content with the memories of the conversation we'd had at dinner about writing. Would I miss his body each night if I slept with him? I knew any act between us that would cause me to want to repeat it was a mistake. I would not be able to count on Norman for anything. His body next to mine night or day. I would have to let go of any thoughts of closeness to him. This frightened me. I wanted my own bed where I felt safe from those fears.

The next morning at 6:00 a.m. the cats jumped on my head. At 10:00 a.m. the phone rang. "It's Norman. I've just taken a swim and am about to read your work. Why don't you come to the hotel for lunch about twelve-thirty?"

"I'd love to, Norman."

At 10:30 a.m. the phone rang. It was Norman. "This piece on your father is very good. I wanted you to know."

"Thank you, Norman."

At 11:00 a.m. the phone rang. It was Norman. "I forgot to mention I have a present for you. I'll give it to you after lunch. I suspect you're going to like this."

"How sweet of you, Norman."

"Don't forget your modeling portfolio and poster. Do you want to meet in the bar or in the restaurant?"

"The restaurant," I said, thinking, *Keep him away from alcohol.*

At noon I got up, still groggy, and headed over to the Bel Air. He was waiting outside the dining room. The maitre d' seated us in the center of the room. He welcomed the attention.

"You look tired," he said proudly. I suspected he felt triumphant about his three orgasms the day before and could have hoped that my fatigue was related to his sexual prowess.

He looked happier.

"When I read your work, why don't you get some sleep? That Daddy chapter is good. Even with your father's illness he sounds like mine. That chapter is very touching." Norman paused a moment. "I hope you brought your modeling portfolio."

"It's in the car."

After Norman finished his lunch of tortilla soup and chicken salad, confessing that he had eaten the same thing the day before, we strolled past the pond to the parking lot to pick up my book of photographs. Walking with Norman was always a stroll. Part strut, part stroll. Sometimes I felt like I was walking with a Mafia chieftain in an outtake from *The Godfather.*

As soon as we entered his bungalow, Norman asked, "Do you mind if I make myself comfortable?" Without waiting for my response, he stepped into the bathroom, his white terry cloth robe in hand. When he came out, he sat in a wing-backed chair in the corner. "Before I read your work, let me have that modeling portfolio," he said, pressing his palms on his knees, his arms straight, his legs spread.

I handed him my pictures and pulled a hassock by his side, then studied him as he studied photographs taken by others who had studied me.

Norman began at the beginning, unlike the way he appraised a writer's manuscript, which he opened to the middle. Slowly he turned each page. His eyes were bright. He fingered the plastic that covered my photographs and did not look at me until he had looked at every picture. He commented throughout, as though he were having a conversation with the photographs.

"The cover of *Newsweek*," Norman said as he opened the portfolio. "I remember that cover. You have the face of the girl next door. The body that contradicts."

"That cover outsold all *Newsweek* covers in the seventies except those on Watergate," I said. "It had been a triple, but the other two girls were told to go home at about 57th Street. The cover was taken at 59th Street in front of the Sherry-Netherland."

"Must be competitive. To be in a triple."

"It's like guerrilla warfare. I had to out-smile them. Know what I was thinking about?"

"Tell me?"

"My father."

"That makes sense. Bet he was proud of you." Norman turned the page. "A *Cosmo* cover. *New York Magazine*. Three covers of you—all in bikinis."

"Advertisers who needed a sexy body but a wholesome face seemed to want to hire me to represent their products."

"My Lord, you were on *Newsweek*, *Cosmo,* and *New York* in the same month!"

"That's the month Warren Beatty introduced himself to me at a party. Then he propositioned me."

Norman laughed. "Those Hollywood stars know their newsstand." He turned a page. *Esquire* and *G.Q.* covers. "Lousy lighting."

"I never liked that cover," I said, turning the page.

"*McCall's*, *Woman's Own* covers. I see you modeled in England."

"For three months. London had great lighting. Overcast skies make terrific photos."

As Norman turned the page, he began to chuckle. "A cover of *Mothers to Be*. That reminds me. Are you wearing a diaphragm?"

"Yes, Norman," I said. "Why aren't you wearing a condom?"

"I feel like a prisoner in one of those things. Trapped. Can't keep my erection. Sorry, luvie."

I frowned.

Norman turned the page to an ad for Fabergé. "'Are you wild enough to wear it?' You were the Tigress girl! I saw your commercial on *60 Minutes*. That controversy. Sex in commercials."

"That's right. The bathing suit didn't have a bra but was fabric woven over my body. It looked like black rope. In the seventies jiggling breasts were considered x-rated."

"How times have changed," Norman said. "Who directed you?"

"Mike Cimino."

"He self-destructed after *Heaven's Gate*, didn't he?" Norman said. "What was he like?"

"Cruel. He told me I wasn't sexy and wondered why the client had hired me. I cried, and all my individual lashes that took one hour to glue on came off. We had to break to glue them back on."

"Did he apologize?"

"Yes, but we ran into overtime, which infuriated him. Again."

"Well, you got your revenge." Norman's attention remained on a photograph of me in Tigress hot pants, bare-chested with my arms crossed over my breasts, chin held high, hair blowing in the wind. "Sexual repression. The seventies. Your beauty caused much controversy. Funny, I didn't know your name, but I knew your photos, these ads."

"In those days models didn't hire publicists."

"Why, you were an original supermodel," Norman said, turning a page. "So it was you who spoke the phrase, 'All my men wear English Leather, or they wear nothing at all.'"

"The commercial ran ten years."

Norman laughed and ran a hand under his armpit, then took a whiff. "I'm one of the ones who wears nothing at all. Yep, that was a good campaign. You told men what to do. Won't work with me, kiddo," Mailer said to the photo as he gave me the elbow.

I turned the page.

"For Tabu you are holding the violin and the man. You tower over him. Had to be on a box," Norman said.

"I was," I said.

"And here we have the famous date with *Esquire* that Buzz mentioned when he introduced us. Lee Eisenberg's opinion of your date. I'll read him later," Norman said with a sigh. "Good photo."

"I liked Lee," I said. "He was nice."

"Fuck him?" Mailer said, chuckling.

"Norman, that's nasty. Of course not."

"Here we have your poster for *Take This Job and Shove It*. My, you have wondrous cleavage, but this MixMaster hairdo makes you look like a sheepdog."

"I like my hair like that, Norman. You're old fashioned," I said.

"With your hair off your forehead you are elegant. Here, in French *Vogue*. This is my favorite look of yours."

"Seems to be the favorite of a lot of people, but I still like my sheepdog hairdo."

"And here—Winston. The Down Home campaign. Lordy, you look so All American. Some body of work," Norman said, laughing, as he closed the book and at last looked at me. "Clay Felker must have loved you."

"I don't know him," I said.

"My dear, he put you on the cover of *New York Magazine* three times."

"I never met a lot of people who hired me."

"Helen Gurley Brown. Didn't she book you for the *Cosmo* cover?"

"No, Scavullo."

"*Newsweek*. Didn't you meet those editors?"

"The cover editor. When the magazine hit the stands, the editors called to meet me."

"What did you wear?"

"Black knit minidress with a drawstring bodice. Black suede knee-high boots. A green velvet cape, Victorian collar."

"You walked into a room of editors, headed by Osborn Elliott, in that getup?"

"Looking sexy was business. Getting attention got the job."

"While they were intimidating you, you were intimidating them. What did those *Newsweek* editors ask?"

"What my parents thought of the cover. I told them my mother thought my hot pants were too short. But my father liked it—though he subscribed to *U.S. News and World Report*."

"I know those editors. I know how they felt. How you felt. What a funny scene."

Norman paused and looked at me, and for that moment I felt my father's presence. My father's approval along with Norman's. My father would have liked Norman...at this moment in time. I loved when Norman gave me attention. I loved that he respected the hard work that modeling had been. I loved that he cheered my success.

Maybe one day I would be able to write a book about my days as a model. Norman would understand all the exploitation in that world. How I viewed modeling as a slaughterhouse of virgins. All those test shots fledgling models had to endure, during which photographers used flattery to try to get the model to undress. Then the sex that followed. Celebrated Italian film director Antonioni touched on this in *Blow Up*. Imagine a book on the modeling industry written by me and edited by Norman Mailer. I think Norman would like that. But would Norman and I last beyond this idyllic summer in 1984? I certainly hoped so.

Chapter 8

Norman had *Tough Guys Don't Dance* with him and had written a poem inside the cover.

"Oh, Norman," I said.

"Read it," he said.

> To Carole,
> Bird, angel, hoyden, shrew
> Witch, bitch, through and through
> Sport, spirit, flasher, sprite
> Some good man is going to treat you right!
> Cheers, Love, Norman (1984)

This poem proved it was impossible to question Norman's intentions. He was going to help me, not abuse me.

Then doubt set in as I wondered, *Was he offering to help me because we'd had sex that he seemed desperately to need? Or did he believe in my writing?*

I wasn't going to analyze his reasons, but then I caught myself doing just that. What if he were helping me because he liked to make love to me and liked my writing? There was nothing wrong with that. Morality has little to do with creativity, the artist, art. My God. There was George Sand. Anaïs Nin had an affair with Henry Miller while she was married. Their affair was their material. Morality had little to do with writing. Then I told myself that I wasn't Anaïs Nin. And Norman Mailer wasn't Henry Miller.

Still, Mailer had six wives. He needed variety to create. Simple. We would be helping each other. We would be giving to each other. Mailer was a philanderer. It was his identity. To love someone is to accept them.

"What do you think I'm gonna do? Kick you out and never speak to you again? What you don't understand is that I'm loyal," Norman would say to me in the years to come. But later the man who wrote, "Some good man is going to treat you right," would kick me out and never speak to me again. Then he would threaten, "If you ever try to write about me, I'll haunt you from my grave."

No wonder Arthur Miller, who wrote *Death of a Salesman,* refused to introduce Norman Mailer to Marilyn Monroe when she was his wife. Arthur Miller understood Norman Mailer.

In 1984, however, I trusted Norman Mailer. His poem proved I could trust him. I was in love with the man, and I was going to follow his advice. He told me to quit acting if I wanted to be a writer. I listened to him.

But I would have to buffer myself against Mailer's many faces, his temper, his entourage of jealous mates and business companions—the "enablers" of Mailer's alcoholism—who would vie for their master's attention. Mailer may not have been a Mafia godfather, but he was the godfather of publishing. "I'm like an old police dog in publishing," Mailer would say. "No one comes near my block."

If I weren't published in three years, I would accept that Norman had been putting me on and that I had no talent.

I dried my eyes as I closed the book on the poem.

"Now, now," Norman put his arm around me. "My lessons aren't for the sensitive, my dear. I'm not always this nice. Make the reader cry, not yourself."

"Yes, Norman." I felt foolish.

"You must work at your craft. Take more classes. Vocabulary."

During Norman's stay at the Bel Air in 1984, I noticed he used words like oxymoron, swath, sententious. Hearing him speak was an education. When I was with him, I felt as though I were in a classroom. I loved listening to him even though he was formal and old-fashioned. My father had been too.

But my father never yelled at me or ridiculed me, which Mailer would do during our lessons. He would shout his criticism and pound on my desk, reminding me of a tyrannical Henry Higgins. He was angry, he would explain, and it was my fault because I had done something stupid or wrong or been lazy. Mailer would justify his rage, most often blaming it on me. For nine years I would believe him.

"You write well about alcoholism," Norman said, placing my stack of manuscripts on the carpet of his bungalow. "I wonder what you were like drunk."

"Cried a lot. Violent. Like you."

"I'll never drink around you," Norman said. "Now let me see that chapter on the flasher." His eyes sparkled. "Are you a flasher?"

"Good Lord, no."

"I'll let you know if I believe you after I read the chapter." Mailer chuckled.

"My professor at U.C.L.A. never asked if I were a flasher. He liked the chapter. His criticism was that I was lazy."

"I don't care what *he* thinks about your work. Let me read it. And I'll give you *my* opinion."

When Mailer read my chapter, he became excited. He appeared to participate in what I described.

It began:

> Whenever I touch cold tile, I remember praying for a bathroom lock. "Privacy. Who wants privacy?" Mom would shout through the door before barging in. She would hold that worn rubber bag as if it were the Topkapi Diamond. "This won't take a second. Get down on your knees and relax. You know you always feel better when it's over." Then she would work that nozzle in and did it hurt! That never stopped Mom. She kept shoving. Soon enough it did fit. Mom knew what was best.

"You bet!" Mailer shouted as he wrote those two words at the end of my paragraph, enthusiastically adding an exclamation point.

"Did your mother do that to you too?" I asked.

"You bet!"

"Did she force them on you?"

"That's right," Norman said with a tinge of anger.

"Then you were sexually abused by your mother. That's according to a Dr. Carnes. He wrote the book on sexual addiction."

"Lots of parents gave their kids enemas."

"If forced, those kids were sexually abused. That's fact."

"We're here to discuss your work, not my asshole. Now this chapter is good. You should turn your five hundred pages of *Picasso Loves Me* into a novel and start with this chapter. Call it *The Flasher*."

"That's pornographic."

"It's telling the reader what your book is about. The purpose of a title. Don't deceive the reader."

"Won't the sex turn off the reader?"

"Listen, kiddo, if someone doesn't like sex, he or she will not like your writing. Don't let our Puritan ethics ruin your creativity. That Pennsylvania Dutch heritage of yours. You must dominate the page. Not let your shame take over."

"This is a lot to digest."

"I must take a nap. The Carson show tapes in two hours. After the taping, would you have dinner with me, say about ten?"

"I'd like that," I said, tweaking his chin as we began to embrace. He pulled away. "Tonight I want you to show your beautiful high forehead. Please don't wear that sheepdog hairdo around me. Your forehead shows your intelligence. You can't be a writer if you want to hide."

"Yes, Norman," I said, walking into the bedroom.

While Mailer did the Carson show, I tried to sleep. Futile. I was nervous when left alone with my thoughts. What was I getting into? What would my mother think of what I was doing? Would she be ashamed? Then I thought, but I'm not living my life for my mother, who denied my father her body. I had to live my own life. Besides, if Mother met Norman, maybe she would understand. I think she would like him. (Years later they would meet. Norman would treat her with respect and would take her to lunch often. Then one day he vanished from her life as he did from mine.)

About 9:30, pleased with his performance, Norman returned. "Shall we go to dinner, my pretty? I'm famished. You look like an Italian countess with your hair off your forehead," he said to me as he rummaged through his closet. "Do you think this goes with this?" He held up a light blue shirt and a navy blazer with gold buttons.

"Yes," I said, wondering why he was asking my opinion.

"Is this tie alright?" He held one with a red paisley motif.

"I think they will look good together," I said.

"Norris helps me decide what to wear," he said, knotting the tie.

Mailer needed someone to make decisions. He was unable to dress because of his insecurity. I was amazed. His need for a wife became apparent.

When we entered the dining room of the Bel Air Hotel during Norman's first trip to L.A., heads turned. Again Norman loved the attention. Romantic dinners in glamorous restaurants seemed to rejuvenate him. Tonight, once more, we were seated in the middle of the dining room, more crowded than at lunch.

"Order anything you want. I'm on an expense account," Norman said. When he was paying, he would encourage me to order moderately priced dishes. He could be a truant officer. Once he denied me a side of string beans.

"Do you think the lobster would be good?" I asked.

"I didn't hear you," Norman said. "Is this restaurant noisier than lunch?"

"Why don't we change tables?"

"Do you think that's really necessary?"

"Yes, Norman. I don't think you realize it, but my voice is loud. We'll have no privacy."

"I'll tell the waiter when I see him."

I thought how peculiar that I had to encourage Norman to assert himself. If he had been drinking, I doubt if he would have been this submissive.

We were given a comfortable booth on the side, away from the harsh light of the chandeliers.

"Oh, Norman, this is much better."

"Better for me as well," Norman said, massaging my thigh beneath the table as I massaged his. "Now, what are you going to have?"

"Lobster."

"Me too."

That evening did we ever enjoy the Random House expense account. After a sampling of caviar, we tore into our lobsters.

"This is a poor imitation," Norman said, cracking a claw. "I will take you to Bangor, Maine. Mount Desert. There we will have real lobster."

"What's special about Mount Desert?"

"I'm beginning my novel there. *Harlot's Ghost*. It's going to be my big book. We'll go mountain climbing."

"I don't think so. That's not my sport, Norman," I said, tossing my salad.

"You'll like it. You're not one of those TV addicts?"

"I like old movies. Talk shows. What time is it?"

"I'll get the check," Norman said. "We have some time until Carson airs. On the show Shelley Winters insists that I met Marilyn Monroe. That irritates me."

"Norman, surely you met her at some point."

"Of course not. Are you doubting me too?"

I shrugged my shoulders and dodged the answer. It seemed impossible for Mailer to have written about Monroe with a sense of awe and discovery if he had ignored her when she had been a starlet. In 1984, I trusted Norman and believed everything he said.

Chapter 9

After dinner Norman and I returned to his bungalow. Instead of going to the bedroom to turn on the television, he sat on the love seat. "Come. Sit by my side," he said, holding my hand, staring into my eyes. He appeared to be on the verge of tears. "I'm going to call my wife. First I want to explain that Norris and I are friends. Our marriage, as far as romantic love is concerned, is over."

"That's sad, Norman," I said, wondering why he had to stay with Norris.

"Our marriage has become dull, boring, but if she should find out about us, I'll never speak to you again. I know it's your nature to be open about your relationships, but will you please do as I ask?"

"Of course, Norman," I said, not realizing that Mailer's threat was preparing me for his exit strategy years later. All he had to do to end our relationship was to say, "Norris found out about us." Even though she had known about us from the beginning.

Yet, this evening, I chose to believe him. He had the ability to sound sincere under the most awkward circumstances. Besides, I wanted to believe him. Quite simply, I had to believe him if I wanted to be in his life. I told myself that he was a great man. I respected his work, his talent. He created words on a page. Words were his way of life, his vocation, at which he was a champion. Surely his spoken word meant as much as his written word—for which he had been so honored. He had written *Some Honorable Men*. With that title he had to know about honor. Norman was trapped in his sixth marriage. He couldn't take paying any more alimony.

Not only did he need a wife to tell him what to wear, he would soon need a wife to care for his aging body. A wife who was a friend. A wife who would not disturb his drinking pleasure. Norman would not divorce again, I thought. No matter how passionately he felt about a woman.

Mailer had enough experience with women to know that sexual attraction had a limited run. Like a Broadway play. He wanted me in his life, but it was too late for him to commit to me. This made me feel inadequate. Less than. But what could I do with my intense feelings for him? These feelings would grow into love, which would consume my life. Make me a prisoner of Norman. His control. His wrath.

I told myself as I was falling under his spell that Norman had never been successful with commitment anyway.

"Why don't you get a divorce?" I asked.

"Ever hear of children?" Norman said. His sadness turned to mild sarcasm. "John Buffalo is six years old."

I didn't push Norman further, though I wondered if divorce would not have been better for all concerned, providing he had been telling the truth. Norman was incapable of marriage, as Gloria Steinem said. He may have gone through the ceremony, but he was incapable of honoring the commitment of a mature partner. He had proven this five times, the absentee father for seven children.

Throughout dinner that evening Norman had been anxious. He had studied the wine list with longing, then ordered a Perrier. I would have to find ways to relax him when we were together. Sex was one way; laughter, another.

Did Norman have a spiritual life, I wondered? He'd written about God, but did he believe? Or did he believe that he had to do it all? Did Norman feel that if he controlled everything and everybody his secrets wouldn't be found out? What was he hiding? What was his secret shame?

I had learned that my secrets had made me sick. Writing about them was one way to get rid of them. In 1983 and 1984, when Norman had read about the awful things I had done, he had identified. He had laughed. If only I could help him to look at himself and to laugh at his own behavior. Sure, he had done this in *The Armies of the Night*, but this did not disclose his deeply guarded sexual secrets. If he could learn to laugh at shame then he wouldn't need to drink to relax from the tension of his conflict.

I was putting Norman's needs above my own. I was focused on fixing him, saving him, rescuing him while I was falling under his spell, a quicksand-like love that would leave me feeling worthless when he was done with me.

Since the night in 1983 when we met, I had begun researching him and his work. During six years of marriage to Beverly Bentley, he had written five books. By 1991 he would have been married to Norris Church for fifteen years and written only three original books—*The Executioner's Song*, *Tough Guys Don't Dance,* and *Ancient Evenings*. Why wasn't he writing more? Was it the parties or the drinking or both? If he were to stop drinking, he would write more and live longer. Parties would lose their appeal because one's values change when one becomes sober. I knew Mailer's big book was in sobriety. Would he ever get there?

Suddenly I realized Norman wasn't the only one with control problems. I was focused on his life instead of my own. That way I didn't have to take responsibility for becoming an adulteress. That's what was happening to me. By trying to save and rescue Norman, I did not have to own up to how I was ruining my life. My reputation. Each time he left me, I felt such pain. Feelings of abandonment. Worthlessness.

If I blamed Norris Church and Norman Mailer, I didn't have to take responsibility for allowing myself to fall in love with a world-class professional philanderer. And for settling for being the "other woman" because I had given up on myself.

That night in 1984, Norman telephoned his wife. He did not ask me to leave the room. He never did. We all knew about each other and accepted the situation for nine years. Not long after Norman and I began our affair, he told me, "Norris knows about us. Wisely she hasn't said anything."

Norris never tried to get to know me, nor did I try to get to know her. The thought did occur to me when I realized there was no sexual relationship between them.

Norris Church and I actually had a lot in common besides Norman Mailer.

Norris Church had taught art to children. So had I.

"In high school I was in all the clubs and the president or secretary of them all," Norris Church said in the Manso biography of Mailer.

So was I. In high school I was the art editor of the yearbook, in the National Honor Society, band, orchestra, cheerleading, Future Teachers of America.

Norris Church worked her way through college. So did I.

"I picked beans one summer," Norris said. "But that was hard work out in the sun, so I went to the Atkins pickle factory, worked there when I was sixteen, seventeen, eighteen. One day the girl on the slicer across from me and I started throwing pickles at each other. The boss saw us, so I was put in the onion room, which is the lowest level of hell. To this day I don't cry when I peel onions.... Six weeks after I finished that job, I slept with my hands under my pillow because I couldn't stand the smell."

At fourteen, I lied about my age and became a soda jerk at a local drug store. At fifteen, I took up waitressing at the local Howard Johnson's where I would pinch ice cream for my father. At sixteen, I graduated to cocktail waitress, and during the winters I served meals in the student cafeteria of Penn State despite a partial scholarship. After graduating from college, I taught art for one year, then became a stewardess for Pan Am and flew around the world. Airsick, I lost twenty pounds. On a medical leave of absence due to weight loss, I began modeling in Paris.

"I'd always had a dream of being a model," Norris Church said. She became one.

So did I. Here we differed. I became a supermodel while Norris Church struggled to get hired.

Norris Church loved powerful men. "I attach myself to people who are on the move…exciting, interesting people," she said.

So did I.

"It's true, in a sense everything I am today is because of Norman," Norris Church said.

Here, we were very different. Though after nine years of our love affair, Norman wanted me to feel and to believe this.

We also differed on issues of having children. Norris Church left her infant son, Matthew, with her parents in Arkansas to move to New York to live with Mailer. She became pregnant, miscarried, became pregnant again, and only then did Mailer marry Norris Church.

In 1975, Claude Picasso became a billionaire when the French government awarded him his share of Picasso's estate. (Picasso had left no will.) Though Claude and I had lived together since 1971, at which time I supported him, and though we became engaged in 1973 when Pablo Picasso died, I did not become pregnant to force a wedding. In 1975, Claude jilted me.

My self-righteousness did not justify my making love to Norris Church's husband. Not much did. Except that I loved him, just as Norris Church loved him when she met him in 1975, and he was living with Carole Stevens, who had given birth to Maggie Mailer in 1971. The revolving Mailer love affairs.

In 1984, Norman and Norris had been together many years. Their sexual sparks had turned into friendship. Because of the way Norman made love to me (and in future years because of the frequency), I suspected Norman Mailer and Norris Church had an arrangement. Their marriage had become one based on economics. And status.

By keeping us apart, Mailer could live two separate lives. Socially, Norris Church would feign annoyance, but I was sure she didn't care. Her posture of vexation was necessary for her to maintain her image. As long as her social and financial positions were secure, she wouldn't cause a confrontation. Norman gave me writing lessons, which was what I wanted from him, as well as his love, which Norris Church and I shared.

And what kind of name was Norris Church? It had been invented by Mailer along with her identity. Her real name was Barbara Davis.

I knew the difficult job Norris Church had being married to Norman Mailer. I didn't want to be imprisoned in a marriage to anyone. Not owned by a marriage contract like chattel. I'd done that. I wanted my freedom. I suspected part of the reason that parties had become so important to Norris Church was that they were an escape from Mailer's demands. Marriage to him was a job. The job I wanted was as a writer. I wanted to make my own money and to make my own love to Norman. When I felt like it. Not night after night.

Who was I kidding? I would have married Norman Mailer in a heartbeat. I didn't have the option. He never asked me. He told me that he couldn't ask me. And I felt flawed because of this. Oh, I feigned that I didn't care, but I cared. The pain was hidden under the indifference.

Because John Buffalo was young when Norman and I met, Norman said, "We need a cover story. I'm going to tell people that you and I met in 1971. I didn't meet Norris until 1975, and in 1971 you were divorcing Ron Mallory. We were both available. I'm going to say that because you were such a bad alcoholic, I stopped seeing you. But now that you're sober, we have become friends."

Would anyone believe Mailer's nasty assessment of me (or as I would come to believe later, a piece of character assassination)? Was this one more example of his self-delusion?

That evening in 1984, after Norman called Norris, he took me into the bedroom of his bungalow at the Bel Air Hotel.

"Does Norris know about that woman you were just with in Chicago?" I asked.

"No," he said. "I've known that woman for twenty years. Once a year we get together."

"How does her husband feel about you?"

"He accepts the situation," Norman said, undressing.

"I think it's terrific you've kept a sexual relationship with a woman for twenty years."

"You do?" Norman said, pulling me by his side on the bed.

"Certainly. It shows a deep friendship and bond. That's love. Fidelity has to be offered. No one believes you're faithful, Norman. It's not part of your identity."

"I'm not sure you'd say that if I were your husband."

"You'll never know," I said, kissing him on his cheek.

"I want you to come to New York this winter," Norman said. "Do you want to?"

"I do," I said, smiling.

Chapter 10

In June 1984, the morning before Norman checked out of the Bel Air Hotel, I left photos of him at the front desk and a letter saying goodbye and how much I enjoyed his visit. In the letter I thanked him for his lessons and the time he spent with me and for teaching me words that I never had used or even had heard. It was important for me to let Norman know that I had been thinking about him. He had needed attention as much as I had, and what could be better for giving this than the written word to a wordsmith such as Mailer. Writing a letter to The Great One showed courage, which I had hoped he would admire. Then I wondered if I had made a fool of myself. When I returned home, there was a message from him on my answering machine. I dialed his suite, eager to hear his voice.

"Hum, hello," Norman said with a southern drawl.

"Norman, did you get my package? I picked up the pictures that I took yesterday."

"Yeah, they're terrific."

"You look mischievous."

"Yeah, yeah. I look like a small movie producer." Norman laughed. "Who's mischievous."

"What about the background?"

"Oh, the background's sensational. We should talk about the background. I'm absolutely dominated by the background," Norman said again in a southern drawl.

I didn't like Mailer's sarcasm, but remained silent.

"Hey, listen, kiddo, I got your letters. You have such a high opinion of me..."

"I wanted to get you a Prometheus. You know, that flower that's beautiful when it dies?"

"Sure do. And the sentence, 'You have the power to quiet the hoyden in me by unleashing her more often between your sheets....'"

"Does that work?"

"It's a fine sentence. Your vocabulary of sexual love is excellent. You see, you're making progress already." Norman laughed.

"I looked up hoyden. Boisterous is the definition."

"No, I didn't mean it that way. A hoyden to me is not boisterous but slightly wild, like a tomboy, but very cute and sexy. And wicked. Like a tough, wicked sprite."

"I feel a bit better now that you clarified it."

"All those words are interrelated. They hold each other up. Hoyden, vixen, sprite. They don't mean the same thing, but they go together."

"I'm signing up for vocabulary at U.C.L.A. tomorrow."

"You're going to fall in love with vocabulary. Get a paperback thesaurus and carry it with you everywhere. When you have nothing to do, spend fifteen minutes reading it, and you'll enjoy it like sheer crazy. Keep a hardcover edition in your car."

"Norman, that's a good idea. I have one here, but I don't use it much."

"Oh, use it. After you get used to using it, you'll find it's so much fun. I can't tell you."

"Is there a sexual thesaurus?"

"A good modern thesaurus will have all the sexual words. Look in the beginning at the preface. See when it was updated. Look up the word fornication and see what they do with it."

"I like to write about sex, but most sex scenes I read seem to be similar."

"I'll give you a tip. You can use any active verb to indicate 'fuck.' He 'tooled' me. He 'socked' it to me."

"And ass is such a terrible word. I try to use derriere. I read in *The Executioner's Song* Gary Gilmore had a wonderful word."

"Bootie," Norman, said chuckling. "It was bootie."

"It's a lovely word, but I don't have a word of my own."

"Come to think of it, you got a real bootie."

"Thank you, Norman. Yours isn't so minor yourself. And you have a bootie obsession. But you see if I try to get clever with it, I get corny or trite."

"Listen, swim in words for awhile. Lick 'em, tongue 'em, live with 'em. I'll call you before Monday, my pet. I'll be in San Francisco for two days then back to New York."

"I love you and your bootie."

"Get that thesaurus!"

The following week Norman called me from New York. He gave me some more writing lessons.

"Hello, Carole? It's Norman. I've been reading some of your work, and there are some things I want to go over with you."

"I'll get a pen."

"What you have to understand in writing is that you have to know what you've created. Because if you have created it, you don't need the fact."

"I don't get it."

"In other words, if you had a friend who had a cat for twenty years. And you go to the friend, and you know the cat...all she has to say is 'so and so died' and that's enough to bring tears to your eyes."

"Oh, I think I get it."

"Here's another lesson. You take a kid who's a young writer who's beginning, and he goes out and has a fabulous night with a girl, and he's writing about it the next day, and he writes, "'I love you," he said. "I love you," she said.' And he says, 'I'm a great writer.'"

"Do I do that?"

"Just listen. He's not a great writer. I mean, the reader reads it and says, 'Oh, Christ!' And throws the book across the room."

"I do get wound up when I write."

"The more emotion you're feeling as you write, the less good it may be. So read it over again when you're in a different mood, and see if it's still there."

"The Claude Picasso chapter was the most recent and most difficult because of emotion."

"It's good. It's better than the other stuff."

"Those three pages where I wrote that Claude didn't give me a painting by his father and asked that I return the Picasso jewelry that his mother gave me. Would you include those pages?"

"Include them."

"Somebody told me, 'Write everything.'"

"Look, if they're not going to read your book, they're not going to read it."

"Are you writing now?"

"No, darlin', I'm raising money for PEN."

"How was your dinner with Mr. Weintraub?"

"It was good. Jerry has lots of ideas about how to raise money. Now don't get tight when you're writing, for God's sake. You wrote in a relaxed mood. Keep it that way. You don't have to change much.... Just tone it."

"What do you mean by tone it?"

"Just listen. Stop writing. Try to write in one mood. Get back to that same mood every day. Which you do very well anyway. Take on your own authority."

"Do I write with authority?"

"Yes, you do, kiddo. You really have your own authority when you work. That's one of the best things you've got going for you. Do you hear me?"

"Yes, I do. I miss you. I've got a surprise for you."

"Okay, okay. I bet you do. Do you, yeah?"

"Don't you want to know what it is?"

"Hey, listen, lovey, I'm sure this phone's bugged from here to Hong Kong so.... You know...*quid ado quid ado*."

"What's that mean?"

"It means they're interested in me. What can I tell you? I'm popular. Anyway you're terrific."

"I'm reading *Ancient Evenings*. I'm on page two-fifty now. I love the images. It's very funny when it's funny. I'm not sure I understand everything."

"You're not supposed to. Just go with it."

"It's funny how you bring the present day into it. When you do the clichéd kind of mother."

"Nefertiti."

"It's beautiful. It's really pretty."

"It's supposed to be pretty. Large parts of it. You'll see. There's an awful lot in it. It goes through a lot of changes."

"I want to get *Marilyn*."

"You'll get them all before you get done. I can tell. I can tell I got a new fan."

What did Norman mean, "Before you get done?" I didn't have the nerve to ask, but instead said, "If you have any extra books, I'll accept them."

Norman laughed. "I might send you one from time to time."

"I miss you, Norman, my professor."

"Okay, all right. The professor tells the student to go to work."

"I give you a big kiss."

"Okay. Bye, bye, angel."

Conversations like this made me feel close to Norman. Over the years I would believe his concern for my health, my journalism, and my mother, who was in her late eighties, would be his way of showing his love and his friendship. (Why, he would even call my mother who lived in Philadelphia when I wasn't visiting her and have chats with her.)

Phone conversations were almost as important to me as making love. I remember waiting by the telephone for his call, and when he said goodbye I knew it wasn't forever. The phone would be our love line. We couldn't always have sex, so we would be forced to talk. Which was second nature to both of us.

Norman would call me from pay phones in Provincetown, on street corners in Brooklyn, in the subways of Manhattan, from airports in Boston, from his publisher, from his agent, from restaurants. He would make me feel that I was the most important woman in his life. We would share common interests: current events, literature, writing, gossip, how to improve our bodies, our minds. He would be my professor and my father and my lover all rolled into one.

Then there were those times Norman would call collect from Provincetown. I wouldn't want to accept those charges, which led to enormous rows. I would shove the phone bills into my diary.

In one conversation in the summer of 1984 Norman was particularly optimistic. "I've got some good news," he said. "I hope it's good news. I'm going to be directing *Tough Guys Don't Dance*."

"So you'll be in L.A.?"

"Yep, and we can be together. Maybe you can help me with casting," Norman said as though he were teasing.

I was happy to help Norman any way I could because he was helping me, and I wanted to be close to him. He also asked me to help him raise money for PEN after he had been elected its president. Mailer wanted to be President of the United States, he once told me. To him, this was the next best thing, and he wanted to do a good job. I wrote some fifty letters to Hollywood celebrities in Norman's name requesting contributions for PEN. Norman knew I had once double-dated with Steven Spielberg and asked that I write to him. I was honored to be helping PEN.

At one point I called an old friend, Martha Duffy, a senior editor at *Time* magazine, and asked her to put a mention in the People section about Mailer's fundraising plan—writers reading from a Broadway stage in the fall of 1985.

"It's for PEN, Martha," I said.

"It's for Norman, Carole," Martha said.

I didn't understand Martha's response. It must have been the way I presented it, I told myself. Surely Norman would make PEN aware of my efforts.

He never did. Martha Duffy, like Arthur Miller, understood Norman Mailer.

It was February, snowy February, 1985.

Since December I'd been living in Manhattan in a sublet off Central Park on West 74th Street belonging to an actor friend. It had eleven rooms, high ceilings, an eat-in kitchen, an exercise room, a cozy den, and a dining room with a long, narrow table that Norman took advantage of when editing my work.

Norman had visited me each week since December. Sometimes we'd meet at restaurants. The Chelsea Hotel, his favorite. Donahue's, he liked because of its dimly lit booths. Gallagher's, I loved because of its lack of pretense and the maitre d' who went out of his way to please Norman. At Shun Lee the maitre d' had no idea who Mailer was or didn't care and called him Mr. Railer. Norman wouldn't go to Rúelles, the restaurant on the corner. Too loud and yuppie, he said. He hated Hunan, also nearby. Café des Artistes, three blocks away, was one of his favorites. We dined frequently at Frankie and Johnnie's too.

"I fucked a girl in the bathroom here years ago," Norman would tell me at each visit to the latter. "Want to see it?"

Each visit I would shake my head and frown.

I knew there was an explanation in Norman's childhood for his desire to have sex in a dirty bathroom. The only one that made sense was his mother's forced enemas, which had to have taken place in a bathroom.

Norman liked games. Acting out, pretending we were characters in a play that we made up as we went along.

He was due any minute. What would I wear this week?

Grabbing my black stockings, garter belt, G-string, and corset, I threw them on. Oh, and the necklace from the Metropolitan that Norman gave me for Christmas. Nefertiti's! I stepped into a pair of black sling-backs and studied my image in the looking glass. I'd forgotten to polish my nails.

Buzzer. Just in time. I ran from the bedroom, listening to my heels clickety clack on the hardwood floors. Practically tap-dancing my way through the den into the living room, I skidded to the door and grabbed the knob for balance.

He knocked.

I opened.

He held a bouquet of red carnations.

"Oh, Norman, for me?"

"You are alone. I presume."

Like a magician's assistant, I stepped from behind the door.

"My, my, what have we here?" Norman said in almost a growl. "Black certainly becomes you, my princess."

"How'd you lose weight, Norman?"

"I have a new diet. I'll show it to you, but you have no need for it." Norman sashayed in a strut to the coffee table in the center of the room. "But now it would please me if you stood by the fireplace and let me appreciate your beauty." Norman laid his coat on the coffee table while I held the flowers in front of me.

"No, no! Don't hide your treasures, my pet."

Norman's baritone voice excited me. He could throw his voice and use it as though it were an instrument. He controlled his vocal chords as he controlled most things in life.

"Now, babe, turn around," Norman said, unzipping his fly.

"DON'T CALL ME BABE!" Dropping the flowers, I kicked off my shoes, marched into the bathroom, undressed, and put on my robe.

When I returned to the living room, Norman was staring off into space. Would he ever understand why I hated being called babe? Perhaps he had trouble remembering names due to memory loss or perhaps not using my name diminished intimacy, which assuaged his guilt. It was all those years having sex with stars who called me babe when they had forgotten my name. But Norman wasn't a star. He wasn't a Hollywood retread. Had I overreacted, I wondered? He was simply an old-fashioned chauvinist. Why was I trying to change him when I loved him?

"The carnations are beautiful, Norman," I said, picking them up.

"You make such an issue of minutiae. Now our day is ruined." Norman looked crushed.

"What about my lesson? I've written a new chapter."

Norman sighed. "Let me see it. You've put me in a foul mood."

"I'm sorry, Norman," I said, kissing him on his cheek.

"I have enough fighting at home. I see you to get away from all that."

Norman held onto the arm of the sofa as he stood. His knees were giving him trouble. "The gout," he would say, frowning.

I led him into the den where he sat down at the captain's desk and turned on the lamp. On the opposite side of the desk there was a window that had a view of the townhouses across the street. I pulled the shade partially down.

"Pull that all the way down," Norman said. He was afraid of people spying on us, even when I lived on the thirty-first floor and had a view of only the Hudson River.

I pulled a straight-backed chair next to Norman and sat beside him.

"You've done a lot, I see," he said.

"You told me it needed a rewrite."

"Let me read," Norman said, raising his bushy eyebrows while lowering his voice. We were over our tiff.

Norman's editing my work gave him a sense of purpose and made him feel that I respected him, which soothed his feelings hurt by our quarrels. I felt valued when he looked at my written words. I could talk to him better through my writing than through our spoken words. This was why I felt so complete sitting by his side while he studied my sentences, syntax, and rhythm. I believed he loved me most when he edited my work. And during those times I knew I loved him.

Chapter 11

For half an hour Norman read. Sometimes he laughed; other times he frowned. He was participating in my text, and once again I was thrilled watching him. He tapped his foot. His mouth moved as though he were reading the manuscript aloud, but he emitted no sounds. His body bobbed back and forth. He put his entire soul into the process of reading.

At last, he put the manuscript aside.

My back ached; therefore, I rubbed his. What I felt, I assumed he was feeling. It was like that a lot.

Norman cleared his throat. "It's getting there. You are still using too many adverbs and adjectives."

"How do I know when to cut them out?"

"Read your work aloud. That will help you make choices."

"I thought I cut them way back."

"Time is a great editor. Read your work the next day. The next week."

Norman looked back at the text. He was tired. I could tell studying my writing sapped his energy. Or had he been up late partying?

"Oh, I just wrote this a few days ago."

"Too recent to be done editing. And be ready to throw all of my rules out if the rhythm supports your choice."

"Rhythm dictates?"

"Rhythm dictates. Always."

"How's my dialogue?"

"You write good dialogue. Probably because of all those years acting. But keep it punchy."

"Like a boxer."

"Like a boxer. Jab. Jab. Jab." Norman punched me in the upper arm.

"Ouch," I said. "Back and forth quickly."

"As fast as possible while still relaying the information. Do not give more than four or five sentences to each response."

"Why's that?"

"The reader will tune out if he has to read speeches."

"Short and snappy?"

"Right. You do it from time to time. Study my edits."

I looked at his corrections on my writing. They made sense. I wrote so quickly sometimes I lost my concentration.

"I see here how you cut my dialogue way back."

"Less is more. And keep your sentences short!"

"Why?"

"You get into less trouble, grammatically speaking. But also for rhythm."

"Short sentences have a rhythm of their own?"

"Yes, they do darlin'. They add energy to writing."

"Right."

"Long sentences slow the forward movement. Don't forget to keep your writing bold."

"Even my sex scenes?"

"Especially your sex scenes."

"What if the reader is repulsed?"

"Then your writing is good," Norman said with a chuckle.

I thought, that's easy for Norman to say. He wasn't a former model who had been called the "It girl" in the seventies. Will I ever be free of the stigma of having been a model? I worried that the reader wouldn't take my writing seriously if I were too bold.

Norman continued, "If the reader is repulsed, you've made him feel. That's what good writing is about."

"But to be repulsed by a sex scene is to be turned off."

"That is not your responsibility, Carole. Your job is to relay secrets. Shame. You're not having a phone conversation or running for office."

"I'm afraid I'll lose the reader if I'm too bold," I said with a frown, feeling like the brazen hussy my mother used to call me when my slip showed in sixth grade.

"You can't write to please the reader all the time. Do you think Henry Miller wrote *Sexus* worrying about how the reader would react to his sex scenes?"

"No."

"Or Anaïs Nin. When she wrote *Delta of Venus*, did she second-guess the reader's reaction to her writing, which was about great sex?"

"Norman, what if people say I'm writing pornography?"

"You can't be a wuss and write about sex, and you must write about what you know, and you know sex. That Warren Beatty chapter was terrific. You took the reader there."

"It didn't embarrass you?"

"Me, dearie, I don't embarrass," Norman laughed and hugged me.

"But Warren is hero-worshipped in Hollywood."

"Good. You're telling the truth about him. How many women has he exploited? He's hardly a saint. You must show the sexual act, not tell it. Do you remember my sex scene in *Ancient Evenings*?"

"About Honey Bee? That was terrific."

"Do you think I worried about embarrassing myself? If the reader is embarrassed that's on him. His choice. But still embarrassment is a feeling and making a reader feel whatever he chooses to feel is the writer's job."

"I hardly think Steinbeck worried about the reader feeling depressed when he wrote about the Great Depression in *The Grapes of Wrath*."

"You've got it, kiddo. Don't be afraid to show warts and all when writing anything. Especially sex. And you write great sex scenes. I rarely edit them."

"What if the reader thinks it's gross?"

"Haven't you gotten it yet? Stop trying to please the reader. Great sex is gross at times. You want to write about things people don't talk about. That's why we write."

I thought maybe one day I'd write about Norman. The sweet side and the cunning side.

"Takes courage to be a writer, Norman," I said.

"Sure does. You can do it."

"It's our Puritan ethic."

"The Pilgrims tried to ruin our sex lives," Norman said, laughing.

"I get so discouraged at times."

"Look at all the rejections I had with *Deer Park*. I put them in my next book! You have to stand behind your work. If you don't, don't expect anyone else to." Norman smiled, then hugged me.

"Next week I want to look at your modeling portfolio."

"Norman, you've been through that book five times." I didn't like that Norman wanted to see my photos again. I was getting the impression that he was just a horny geriatric.

"Your modeling book is an insight into you and your novel. How you attracted those stars relates to your beauty. Some of those guys must have been aware of what you looked like before they met you," Norman said.

"Warren Beatty had seen me on the newsstand in March 1971. I was on three covers that month."

"That's what I mean."

"What's that got to do with my novel?"

"He was turned on by your beauty, kid. He had met you on the newsstand while you had met him in movies. But before you met him in the flesh."

"I never thought of it like that."

"You were the star of the newsstand that March. Look, use those ads, those photos, to sell your novel, instead of their products. You're going to have to be very careful with the publicity on a novel about a female flasher. Why don't you tell the press you were addicted to having sex with movie stars?"

"But I'm writing fiction."

"Perhaps the press won't nail you as a flasher if you talk about Bobby De Niro or Sean Connery. Why don't you tell me a bit more about what they were like?"

Norman was obsessed with the stars I had dated. Over the years he would grill me about their sexual techniques, prowess, and physical endowments. I had the impression that Mailer envied my experiences.

"Norman, you make me feel like you're using me."

"My dear, I'm not a Hollywood wolf. I'm an old man who writes. You will get this novel published. I'm trying to help you with the press. Maybe you should study your modeling portfolio more often."

"I'd rather write." I yanked the sash on my robe. "What should I work on next week?"

"You know, I think Scott Meredith would handle you if you wrote a book about porn stars."

“Stop treating me like an object!”

“But you’ve been one all your life,” Norman said, chuckling.

“That’s not funny. I’m trying to write about having BEEN that. Norman, you have this thing about flesh. Sometimes I think you’re carnivorous. Flesh is a wrapper. My novel’s about becoming a free spirit.” I wondered if publishers would view my novel simply as a dirty book and exploit me further. Instead my book was about exploitation in Hollywood. Would I be further victimized if I were published by the wrong publisher and my book were promoted like a tawdry sex book?

“Good luck making that point.”

“I tried marriage. It’s silly. Business. Marriages should be on the stock market. Mini-corporations. Look at yours!”

“Leave my marriage out of your writing.”

“Your marriage is your problem. I’m tired of this conversation.”

“My marriage is not a problem.”

“Then what are you doing here?”

“Editing your novel.” Norman’s face was flushed. Norman was adamant about protecting his marriage, which I viewed as a charade. Most people who knew Norman knew he had had several mistresses.

“Gordon Lish’s and Margaret Atwood’s classes are helping me. Can you see the improvement?”

“Lish teaches a writer’s voice. You don’t need him.”

“Lish read some of my writing about my father. Those chapters you read when we met. He said I should be writing nonfiction. ‘With the experiences you’ve had.’”

“Nonfiction is too hard. Start with this novel.”

“He said there was nothing wrong with my writing that an editor couldn’t fix. He said he edited Raymond Carver. He said he made Raymond Carver’s writing.”

“Don’t believe everything Lish says. When you’re ready for nonfiction, I’ll let you know.”

“Lish said you want me to write fiction so that I won’t write about you,” I closed my eyes and puffed out my cheeks, prepared for his response.

Lowering his voice, Norman said, “When you’re ready to write nonfiction, I’ll give you a letter authorizing you to write my biography. Now, I’m hungry.”

(In 1991, Mailer would give me this letter, but this was because he felt he could control me and get press at the same time. He would not have allowed me to write the truth.)

I kissed Norman on his cheek, then turned to go. "I'll make lunch."

"Okay," he said. Arguing stimulated Norman. "I think you need some writing direction. While you're doing lunch, I'll do that."

I scurried to the kitchen. I grabbed the basket filled with apples, bananas, pears, kiwis, blueberries, strawberries, and grapes and carried it to the dining room. A deep purple cloth covered the table. Dropping my robe, I crawled on top with my fruit basket. Recalling Goya's *Naked Maja*, I imitated the pose, then spread the fruit around, under, and over my naked body, then sang out, "Norman, lunch time."

Norman's face shone bright like a little boy's with a new toy. "My, my what have we here?" he said holding onto his belly as though I was his new meal. "You look like Linda Darnell. But you're too young to remember her. She was a great beauty like you, my sweet."

"Thought you deserved a treat for all your hard work," I said, eating a grape. My body ached from the wooden table, but I didn't mind because it was more important to give pleasure to Norman. I knew he felt old, but he still had sex appeal, for me anyway.

He took off his clothing and ran his hands over my body. "I like that you surprise me, but, my dear, I am too large to get on that table with you. Shall we go into the bedroom?"

He held out his hand and helped me off of the table as he picked up a strawberry. "Let's take some of this fruit with us," he said.

When we got to the bed, he wanted me to devour the grapes and him. Simultaneously.

After we made love, we napped. When he left, I went into the study to read his editorial suggestions.

I read Mailer's notes and wondered, "How would Norman and I break up? Would we? I believed in living in the now and thought he would always be in my life. I trusted him. "I'll take an insurance policy out for you," he said later on. "Let me talk to my agent, Scott Meredith. He needs time to investigate these possibilities."

Still, time passed, and there was no policy. I would worry each time Norman left that I would never see him again. Such a loss, such sadness. What would happen to me? He told me I had to quit acting if I wanted to be a writer. Like a fool, I listened to him. I had supported myself with my acting.

I sat on the sofa and clutched his notes to me. Why did I have to fall in love with a married man? I knew I made this choice, but it was painful each time he left. I cried. What did Norris Church have that I didn't have? Besides Mailer. A son, that was who she had. I was barren. Used up. That's what was wrong with me. Men could have experiences with many women and be considered a Romeo, a great lover. Norman loved that I had been with many stars, at least he told me that, but still he preferred a mother to a lover.

My tears were staining his notes to me. I carefully wiped the precious paper. A testimony of his love. How long could this go on? I wasn't going to think about that. He wouldn't just walk out the door on me. No, he had character. He may have lived with Norris, but he loved with me. Still, why did he stay with Norris? He told me he was so unhappy with her. "She has too much on me," he would repeat.

Then I remembered Norman asking me to go to a gay porn film with him.

"That's not my thing," I said.

"Norris goes with me," he said.

"Then go with Norris," I said.

Norris supported Mailer's bisexual side while I did not. His secret shame.

Had Norris Church and Norman Mailer been a "swinging" couple? Was I just one more swing in their open marriage?

One night, Norman wanted me to see Norris in a play at the Actor's Studio. *Strawhead*. About Marilyn Monroe. He had left my name at the box office. I would have to go alone.

As I sat there watching the stunning Mrs. Mailer perform, I thought, *Norman, you are helping her with acting, but she's not an actress. She's a painter. Are you just trying to make her into what you want her to be?*

Was he doing this to me? Trying to make me into something of his creation? But I had wanted to be a writer. I didn't get pregnant like Norris and end up his wife with nothing to do but be his empty vessel. A former pickle and onion factory worker who became an empty socialite vessel because of Mailer's clout. Was Mailer's desire to shape the lives of the women he loved related to a latency issue? Did he feel part of that woman when he helped to create her new career and new name?

My thoughts returned to the play. Norris Church Mailer pulled down her dress and showed her breasts in front of a celebrity audience that Mailer had gathered to witness this spectacle. Later Mailer would say Norris wanted to do it. She stood there so triumphant. Brazen. How could Mrs. Norman Mailer want to embarrass herself and disrobe in front of their friends? Or did Mailer direct this? Was this his idea? Was this another latency act orchestrated by Norman Mailer, and once again Norris was the vessel?

After the play I went home and had a nightmare about Norman ending our love affair with a phone call that Norris had just found out about us. In my dream he hid behind her skirt. He was directing the breakup and using Norris as a cover.

As it turned out, my nightmare would come close to predicting the future.

Chapter 12

In June of 1985 my swap of my apartment with an actor friend who had lent me his in Manhattan had come to an end; therefore, I returned to my apartment in Hollywood. I was in the midst of writing *Flash*.

In July Norman flew from New York to San Francisco to promote the paperback of *Tough Guys Don't Dance*. He arranged that I would fly up from Los Angeles and meet him at the St. Francis on Union Square. We would be spending several nights at this romantic hotel, once again on his Random House expense account.

When Norman arrived in San Francisco, he telephoned me in Los Angeles with directions.

"Enter on Geary Street," he said. "There will be a letter from me at the first desk on the right. Go through the hotel to the main building. I'm on the eleventh floor, room 1140, in the tower."

The lobby of the St. Francis, with its cathedral-like ceilings, towering palms, oversized sofas, art deco lamps, and pianist playing a baby grand, was as glamorous as my memory of the film *Grand Hotel*, yet more seductive.

I picked up Norman's letter. "I'll meet you in the room at 5:00 p.m. Welcome, Herbert." Norman had begun using my father's name as an alias.

I thought Norman using my father's name was more silly than sweet and never confronted him with its negative implications. Norman's temper was violent if he didn't get his way. His tantrums could be unpleasant. I found it easier to say yes or to look the other way when he did things I didn't like. Because I was a little afraid of him, I allowed him to bully me. I studied books on assertiveness training to no avail.

That night at the St. Francis was to be our romantic holiday. No checking his watch for deadlines. No running to the subway to return to Brooklyn for dinner.

I followed the porter who carried my bags to Norman's suite. The bed was king-sized and covered with a white satin bedspread. In one corner there was an armoire with a mirrored door. Burgundy carpet, wall-to-wall. As I began to unpack, Norman walked in.

We embraced. We never had a passionate greeting right away. Because of Norman's age, generally he was only able to have one orgasm; therefore, we would plan when we would make love.

"When did you arrive?" he said.

"About fifteen minutes ago," I said.

"How was the flight?"

"Up and down. An hour."

"I've booked a table at the hotel's restaurant. It's a marvelous view. I think you'll like it."

"I want to be with you, Norman. It could be Chock full o' Nuts."

"Did you bring *The Flasher*?"

I handed him my completed one hundred pages.

After Norman ordered grapefruit juice for us, we sat at a small desk, our bodies touching as he read. When he would identify with passages, he would squeeze my thigh. Reading my work was highly pleasurable for me, though we never spoke about this. It wasn't the subject matter of my writing. It was because Norman reminded me of my father working at his desk when I had been that child playing with my paper dolls at his feet.

While Norman read my work, he felt fulfilled and respected, clearly dominant. His ego was reinforced by my pleasure in being submissive, though the observer in me was studying him at the same time. When Norman read, he reminded me of a giant sewing machine, foot pedal and all. He tapped a foot, mumbled, spurted saliva. He bobbed his torso back and forth. He smiled when my writing worked. Little could distract Norman when he read.

After reading the last page, Norman placed his palm on my manuscript and said, "I like the consistency of this writing. I'm going to give you a letter supporting your novel."

"Thank you, Norman," I said, kissing him on his cheek.

"But if people know we're together, my words will mean nothing. People will think I've written your work."

"How could they?" I said. "Your voice is so different. So formal."

"You don't know the publishing world, my dear. We must keep our affair private for your career and for my family."

"My mother needs to know."

"You can tell her and your sister, but that's it. If I ever left Norris, it would be like bombing a small town." Norman had a pained expression. "You and me, kid, are a hot item, don't you realize? If we make the papers, Norris will be crushed. I couldn't leave Norris if I wanted to."

I didn't understand the mystery of Norris Church's hold on Norman. I understood that after paying alimony to five wives, Norman was unable to do it again, but Norris Church's hold on Norman was more than financial and seemed to be based not just on their young son, John Buffalo. The only conclusion I could draw from a remark like the above was that Norris Church knew things about Norman that he did not want revealed.

After Norman and I were together for eight years, and I had interviewed him nine times, he would say, "You're learning too much about me."

The conclusion I came to was that Norris Church, who Norman had said had gone to gay porno films with him, knew he was bisexual. That was the only thing, it seemed to me, that could account for their close bond.

Mailer's work and Mailer, the man, were a cottage industry. Several publishers had a vested interest in him and his work; his macho image had to be maintained for business and possibly for his own sanity.

Hoping to get the conversation away from his marriage, I asked Norman, "What are you going to write about my novel?"

"Stop looking for compliments, my dear. I love that part of you that laughs at yourself, but I detest the child in you who needs attention."

I knew any letter Norman wrote supporting my novel was in part a way of protecting his family and his lifestyle, but because of the thoughtfulness he put into his writing, I believed he meant the words he wrote.

He wrote about my novel, which he called *The Flasher*, "I think your writing is wicked and funny and marvelously penetrating about matters in sex which are usually seen as promiscuous and perverse."

In my novel I was trying to show the cause of my heroine's compulsive sexual behavior, which took the form of masturbation. Norman had written that this act performed with hostility was "usually seen as perverse"; however, once my heroine understood the origin of her shame and the anger behind her compulsive behavior, she was freed of it. She was able to laugh at herself and that aspect of society that belittled this act. Her shame turned to laughter at her own guilt for an act that was as natural, cleansing, and healthy as bathing.

At twenty-nine, plied with alcohol and marijuana, I experienced my first lesson in masturbation under the direction of Warren Beatty, which Norman had read about. Not only was twenty-nine late to learn about one's body, but from that night on I developed a dependency on drugs and alcohol in relationship to sex. The Beatty chapter was about the relationship between sex, drugs, and alcohol, which had become an addiction for me.

While reading the Beatty chapter in the winter of 1983, Norman had laughed. Six months later, while reading the first chapter about the flasher, Norman had laughed. Later Norman would tell me he had written "marvelously penetrating" in his blurb because he had identified.

In the fall of 1985 I mailed Gloria Steinem my novel. When I wrote Steinem, I told her that Norman had said that she would hate my book, but that I wanted Gloria Steinem's opinion from Gloria Steinem.

Within one week she returned the manuscript, and I thought she had hated it. In my mind Mailer was always right. Trembling, I opened the parcel, which arrived via messenger from *Ms. Magazine*. Steinem began by thanking me for sending her *Flasher*. Then she wrote that, "It was fast, smart, and irresistible to read."

I stopped trembling.

She also wrote that the trouble with Mailer was that women find it too easy to know what he's thinking, and he finds it too hard to know what women are thinking. This is why he can be a very good writer and still not create believable characters, she said. Steinem felt that was sad.

Agreed.

When I told Norman that Steinem had written her support of my novel, he said, "I didn't think Gloria liked sex. Guess that shows you I don't know anything about women."

After Norman read what Steinem had written, he rewrote his blurb. He added, "We see a woman grow despite her sexual foibles, and yet because of them. The sort of feat that keeps one alive."

I suspected Norman's motivation for this rewrite was his desire not to be viewed as a sexist. If his original blurb were placed next to Steinem's, he appeared to be the lascivious old man of literature. By adding a sentence that acknowledged my heroine's growth, Norman protected his image, which was everything to him. Gloria Steinem knew and understood the real Norman Mailer.

Like the three-piece suits Norman wore on most occasions—whether or not one was appropriate—Norman cherished formality. So did his father, Barney Mailer. "My father was terribly elegant," Norman told me. "When I was a child, not only did he wear blue pinstriped suits and a vest, but he wore spats. Pearl-grey spats. A cane. A felt homburg."

"Who was the head of your family?" I asked.

"My mother was the center of it. It was a nuclear family. My father was one of the electrons. A very dapper electron. He was an accountant and didn't have a great deal of money. If he'd had money, he would have been a Beau Brummell."

Norman wore his three-piece suits to the dining room when we stayed in hotels. Not only did he dress like his father, but because he was usually on an expense account, he had the sense of unlimited funds that his father never had. The younger Mailer, with his mistress by his side, could imagine being the Beau Brummell that he wished his father could have been.

"My father was a man who never came to terms with the world," Norman told me. "He was a great romantic. And women adored him because he had the gift of speaking to each of them as if she were the most important woman he'd ever spoken to and as if everything she said was of inestimable value. He didn't fake it. He believed it. He loved it. He adored women."

"Did your parents ever fight?" I asked Norman.

"When I was twelve, my mother wanted to leave my father," Norman said. "Every time there was a fight some big change happened. I grew afraid of change. My mother said she would stay with my father if that's what I wanted..."

"What did you say?"

"I asked her to stay, and my father continued to make her life miserable."

The young Mailer watched and lived with his mother's torment. Some part of Norman must have felt responsible for her suffering. But his primary identification, of course, was with his father. Is it surprising that Norman would abuse the women he loved? That his literature is filled with violence? That a woman was decapitated by his muse in *Tough Guys Don't Dance*?

Barney Mailer had been a gambler. Unsavory members of the underworld harassed him to collect debts he owed—a regular part of Norman's childhood.

Is it surprising that as an adult Norman Mailer would be attracted to criminals in life and in literature? *Oswald's Tale*, *The Executioner's Song*, *Harlot's Ghost*. Jack Abbott.

When Norman identified with his father, I thought he was the abuser of women and consumed by guilt. When Norman identified with his mother, he was his father's victim.

Barney Mailer was a weak man. "One of her electrons," Norman had said. Young Mailer had been let down by both parents. While his mother doted on him and instilled in him the belief that he could accomplish anything, he was afraid of her.

Could the philandering that bonded Mailer to his father be a way for Mailer to punish women?

Whether it was a formal dinner or five hours with his mistress, I felt Norman had to return to his wife and be confronted with the emotional recall and the conflict of his childhood.

"After I leave you, I have to spend time in a bar before going home," Norman would tell me. "This is not easy for me. I wish you would try to understand my position."

I believed infidelity kept Norman caught in his conflicted childhood, which was disturbing because his family had once been whole. Norman's role model for the comfort of a family was conflict. Norman's infidelity guaranteed his reliving the interaction between his mother and his father. Though it must have been painful for the young Mailer to live with the fighting and the drama, I felt this behavior bonded him to his parents.

Norman needed mistresses because his father needed mistresses, but he also needed a wife who would allow him to treat her as a mother figure. I believed Norman was powerless over his infidelity unless he sought help.

After he stabbed Adele, the doctors said he needed to go to Alcoholics Anonymous. Norman refused. He liked his disease and his addictions too much to do anything about them. He was addicted to philandering. I tried to love him as he was and hoped one day he would be free of the ghosts from his childhood, as I hoped one day to be free of mine.

I would take him to the occasional meeting when he agreed to come, but this was a struggle. I had my own addictions to overcome. Trying to rescue men was one of those addictions.

In my interviews with Norman in the coming years, I would address issues dealing with his infidelity and his alcoholism. For our first interview with *Elle* magazine, Norman was concerned that he portrayed his father as a weak man. He asked my permission to rephrase his responses dealing with Barney Mailer.

When Norman read in my manuscript that during my modeling years I had tried to use my beauty to protect my father from the laughter of others, Norman said that he understood. He protected his father with his language, his art.

Whenever Norman and I stayed in a hotel, we enjoyed each meal in the formality of its dining room, and we delighted in dressing up for each other. I was acting as I had with my father, and I felt he was acting as though he were his father. We made each other feel whole.

For Norman's birthday on January 31, 1985, I had given him a red paisley tie. Whenever we went to dinner, Norman would wear the tie as he did that first night in San Francisco.

We were seated at a table by the window with a panoramic view of the city, yet a candelabra blocked our view of each other.

"Can't stand when they put these things on tables." Norman pushed the candelabra to one side. "Now I can enjoy your beauty. You remind me of Joyce Carol Oates." Norman lowered his voice. "But you look like a stripper."

"I'd rather look like Joyce Carol Oates," I said. "Last night you told me I looked like the Mona Lisa."

"In the bedroom. It's your half smile."

"Are you saying the Mona Lisa looks like a stripper?"

"Giving you a compliment about your beauty is like flattering Helen Keller...." Norman laughed. "Haven't you ever won a beauty contest?"

"Lost a few."

"Miss Pennsylvania?"

"And Miss Penn State."

"That's a huge student body. Why'd you lose?"

"My sorority nominated me. We were all paraded around on campus on floats. They voted. Could we order?" I didn't want to recall the event.

Norman signaled the waiter. He wanted steak. I chose lobster.

"I'm trying to understand how a college beauty contest is conducted." Norman buttered more bread.

"After the parade, the finalists had to answer questions in front of the entire student body in the gymnasium."

"That should have been easy for you. You're terrific in front of a camera."

"I froze."

"What was your question?"

"'What was the most challenging event for you to overcome?'"

"And...?"

"I said, 'My father's lobotomy.'"

"Perfect answer," Norman said.

"Not for the judges. Twenty thousand people were silent. I'd wanted to win for my father, but somehow losing made sense. I'd always felt like a loser." I stopped eating and looked into Norman's eyes.

"But you went on to do all that acting. Made it on all those magazine covers."

"I felt like a failure until I got sober. At thirteen I had more self-esteem than at twenty."

"Don't use those words. Psychobabble," Norman said as he added butter and sour cream to his baked potato.

"You hate the word because you have no self-esteem. Ego isn't self-esteem."

"Have it your way, my stubborn one. Have you always identified with your father?"

"Probably."

"Drinking, drugs, and sex could have been your way of deteriorating along with him. How long did he live after the lobotomy?"

"Twenty years."

"What was he like in the end?"

"Crawling around on all fours. Weeding, his only pleasure."

"I don't understand."

"Stopped his twitching. When he was weeding, for the moment he had peace."

"Must have been a horror. People don't understand suffering to that extent. They shut down when made aware of it. Sounds like Tourette's syndrome." Norman pushed his salad to one side.

"Tourette's doesn't affect the mind. The twitching and ticks are similar. Anyway, that was my last beauty contest."

"Then you went on to model and act. More competition."

"Guess I'm counterphobic. I was never nervous in front of the lens, but I've always been terrified to talk to people. The sorority that nominated me had rejected me two years before."

"Why?"

"Couldn't talk to a room full of women. I couldn't make small talk. Neither could my father."

"You're a late bloomer. Typical Capricorn."

"Says the analytical, socially acceptable Aquarian." I squeezed lime into my Perrier.

"Answering that question in front of twenty thousand was a horror."

"I'll just have to turn you into an interviewer so that you can ask the questions." Norman smiled as he sliced his Chateaubriand.

I had never thought about this as a career. This was Norman's idea and a good one at that. He would teach me how to do an interview and would help me to get to celebrities. While he let me down on many promises, he did keep his word about turning me into an interviewer.

Over the years I interviewed many famous personalities, including: Isabella Rossellini, Mikhail Baryshnikov, Lieber and Stoller, Joseph Kennedy II, Kurt Vonnegut, Joseph Heller, Erica Jong, Jay McInerney, Chevy Chase, Dudley Moore, Milos Forman, Gore Vidal, James Ivory, Michael Apted, Lord David Puttnam, Julian Lennon, Mrs. Vincent Astor, Jesse Jackson, and Norman Mailer nine times. Some of these celebrities I had known from Hollywood and some I met through Norman and some I queried with my tear sheets from my more successful interviews.

With each interview, my clout as a journalist grew and so did the use Norman Mailer could make of my skills, my connections with garnering publicity, and my place in the journalistic marketplace—that is the magazine world—a world unto its own.

Chapter 13

The next morning over breakfast, while pondering the beauty of the San Francisco Bay outside our window, Norman said, "I would like to take a drive through Northern California. My friend has a marvelous home on a beautiful lake. He's out of town, and I have the key. We can be alone and make love by the lake."

I was eager to see this special home. A new adventure. Norman was always thinking of new ways to make love. New locations.

For our trip Norman rented a full-size sedan. "I like a big car. Something under me," he said as we drove across the Golden Gate Bridge.

"What do you drive in Provincetown?" I asked.

"An old car."

"What kind?"

"My dear, you know I don't like these questions." Norman preferred that I knew only those things about him that he told me. Later, I discovered he owned a vintage Mercedes.

"We're going to drive by the ocean. I think you'll like the view."

"How long a drive?"

"Three hours."

"It's 10:10 now. We'll be there in time for lunch."

Norman nodded. "Do you like to fuck in places?" he said, smiling.

"I like to fuck in people," I said, not smiling.

"Don't be self-righteous." Norman dug into his pocket for change for the toll. "One day I want you to meet my daughter Susie. She lives in South America."

"Why Susie?"

"She's a psychiatrist. I think you would enjoy talking with each other."

"Let's visit her."

Norman laughed. "I don't know how to get you together. I'll find a way." Norman was showing his conflict in trying to appear faithful. He took a childlike pleasure in solving the problem of having to deceive, even though the solution involved further deceit. These feelings bonded him to his adulterous father.

Norman became quiet and concentrated on his driving in heavy traffic as we headed for the Golden Gate. He had wanted me to be part of his extended family. Susie's mother, Bea, was one of my favorite Mailer wives because she had been a writer.

I liked to ask Norman about his wives, and he liked to tell me about them as though they were old friends. They were all part of the process of loving Mailer. Each one had helped Norman and had added to his talent in her own particular way. He was a handful. Born on the wrong continent. He should have been a sultan. Playing sultan was one of his favorite sex games. No, his lifetime was too much for one woman. Each of his wives had contributed to his writing as he gave of himself. He had used their lives as material, but what were their stories in the struggle to love Norman Mailer?

Sometimes I imagined his ex-wives as five women huddled together, whispering deep in shadow in a German expressionist painting that could have been done by Edvard Munch. Too afraid and too beaten down to speak up. Wanting their identity, yet fearing any mention of Norman's name would destroy the opportunity for the new life that divorce offers.

Why does a man's fame subjugate a woman in society's eyes? Pulitzer Prize winner and National Book Award winner Norman Mailer had stabbed his wife, Adele Morales, and had gotten away with it. When will women count? I wanted to hear what Norman's wives had to say.

"What do you think would happen if all your wives were in one room?" I asked him.

"There would be a party," he said, chuckling.

I had the idea to do a book on Mailer's women. "They all won't talk to you," Norman said. "Norris would. Carol might. Adele wouldn't. Jeanne Campbell would think you're common." Norman chuckled again. "If it makes you feel better, she thinks I'm common. Bea probably wouldn't talk. Beverly, no way. Besides, I'm not famous enough. After I'm dead."

"Why are you certain Norris would agree to be interviewed by me?" I wondered if Norman controlled Norris to that degree or did he believe she liked publicity as much as he did.

"Norris is tough. From sharecroppers. A little southern town where no one wants to see anyone get ahead. She's proud of being married to me and not afraid to talk about it to anyone."

"How did you get with Carol Stevens?"

"Five years, every Monday, I fucked her. Then Beverly left me, and I was lonely. I can't be alone. Never been able to be."

"I felt lonely when I was married," I said.

"I know what you mean."

"Today, living alone, I'm seldom lonely."

"I sense that about you." Norman paused for a moment. "Anyway Carol Stevens and I tried to live together. Good the first six months. Then bad. Lasted three years."

I watched a relaxed Norman talk about his relationships with other women. I was flattered that he felt comfortable enough with me to reveal his feelings. This was not easy for him. Norman's talking about his past made me feel more a part of his present and helped me to try to understand him.

I thought about how difficult it must have been for Bea to be married to Norman during his success with his first book, *The Naked and the Dead,* when he was drinking heavily. For nine years I looked forward to meeting Bea's daughter, Susie. When Norman did go to South America to visit her, he brought me two tiny Peruvian cloth dolls.

When Norman brought me gifts of dolls or fire-engine red plastic makeup kits from his trips to Italy, I was reminded of that part of him that might have thought of me as a tenth child. Possibly this was part of the reason he used my father's name, Herbert, when he left messages. Today, whenever I look at those two cloth dolls, I think of Susie, whom I never had the opportunity to meet.

Norman held his palm over the horn and yelled, "Put your turn signal on. Idiot!" He missed hitting a speeding Corvette. "Goddamn cowboys!"

"Relax, Norman." His face was crimson. With his rage he could have a heart attack. I thought how enmeshed I was becoming in a married man's life. I was more concerned with Norman's well-being than my own. "I'm worried that I'm too much in love with you, Norman. Should I stop seeing you?"

"I'll never stop seeing you." Norman's expression was sincere. Like his father, Norman had the gift of making a woman feel as though she were the most important woman in his life…when he wasn't provoking or subjugating her. He cleared his throat, pushed his chin upward and said, "You're one of the five best lovers I've had. And I've had a lot. You weren't so good when I met you."

"Is that supposed to be a compliment?"

"I always marry women who are good fucks, but this time I'm going to wait."

"Why do you say such things?"

"I need time with a woman. You have to give me time. I'm going to have my sperm count checked."

I stared out the window at the cars whizzing by. Did that mean Norman was thinking of marrying me? Did he need me to become pregnant to get out of his marriage? I decided he was feeding me a line. "I'm going to try to forget you."

"Thirty years ago I would have married you, but you wouldn't have married me."

"You wait. I'll get you jealous."

"I don't get jealous."

"Baryshnikov might be a way."

"Instead of fucking him, you should interview him."

Norman fiddled with the car's radio. "So how'd you meet Baryshnikov?"

"At an art gallery opening last spring."

"Just like that?"

"I was talking to Mike Nichols, and Misha came over to Mike, who introduced us."

"That's right. You dated Mike. So what happened to Baryshnikov?"

"He invited me to his home for dinner and to the ballet a few times. We are just friends." I paused and looked at a poker-faced Norman. "Thought you didn't get jealous?"

"Who says I'm jealous?"

"I don't ask you what you do with that woman from San Francisco you've been seeing for years. Or that woman in Chicago. Women are a game to you. You don't love me. You love intrigue."

"I love you, but not completely."

"You told me not to use adverbs."

Norman laughed.

"You told me you loved me twice in L.A."

"I loved you then," he said wide-eyed, then rolled his eyes. "I can see I'm not going to live that one down."

"You also told me on March 11th that you loved me."

"How'd you know it was March 11th?"

"It's written in my diary."

"Dear Lord, are you keeping one of them?"

"You've turned me into a writer, Norman. Writers write."

"What if your novel doesn't sell?"

"Worrying about 'what ifs' gives power to fear. It'll sell if it's God's will. I don't understand why your illustrious agent, Scott Meredith, turned down my novel without encouraging me to improve it. He wrote that I should begin a new project."

"The Meredith Agency isn't for you."

"A year ago, Norman, you tried to get them to handle me. Why aren't they helping me if you recommended my work?"

"Ask Scott Meredith, not me. How did you get to Gloria Steinem?"

"I sent her some of my work. Jealous that a woman should like my work?"

"Don't be ridiculous. You should write Francoise Gilot and ask for a settlement from Claude. He treated you badly."

"Now you're in my life. After that poem you wrote, 'Some good man is going to treat you right,' I feel safe. Most of the time. Claude and that pain are the past. You make me happy. Even when you roar."

Norman roared like a lion, chuckled, then put his hand on mine. "When I saw Francoise Gilot and Jonas Salk at that benefit in May, he commented on how much he liked you."

"Jonas knew I had a drinking problem. He tried to get me to stop taking Valium. I thought, 'He invented the polio vaccine. What's that got to do with Valium?' My denial was ruling me."

"I don't take pills," Norman said.

"Only Fiorinal."

"On occasion." Norman coughed.

"Anyway, one night I saw Betty Ford on TV, saying she used to take Valium and wine and that the combination kills. Coma time. I thought, 'Look what being a President's wife did to that poor woman,' as I reached for my Valium and wine."

Norman laughed.

"I couldn't identify with a first lady. I wasn't ready to be helped. Jonas tried. He's a kind man."

"He remembered you. 'What a lovely girl you were,' he said. I told them you'd stopped drinking. No wonder he seemed so pleased. You should try writing Francoise. Maybe she'll give you a Picasso or two."

"Fat chance. I'd rather make my own money."

"I think you should sue Claude."

"There's no law about being jilted by a Frenchman you supported when he was penniless."

"So if palimony isn't possible, sue him for something else." Norman thought a moment. "Slander?"

"You talk as though you're always sued."

"Only by Beverly. Let's get off the subject, shall we?" Norman cleared his throat. "Are you reading O'Hara?"

"*Appointment in Samarra*. Can't find a copy of *BUtterfield 8*. Out of print."

"Go to the library. Don't be lazy!"

Norman rolled down the window and inhaled northern California. "This is going to be a big year for me."

"Why did you take me to Bar Harbor in April? Was I research for your novel?"

"I wanted to be with ya, kiddo. I like ya." Norman placed his hand on mine. "You climbed Beehive Mountain better than I thought you would."

"Why did you bring a briefcase to Maine with only a deck of cards and a Hershey bar inside? You're that into appearances?"

"Solitaire helps my impatience. I needed an empty briefcase for notes for my novel."

"You mean you filled your briefcase with notes about our three days?" So am I in *Harlot's Ghost*?"

"Nope. It's a big bosomed woman."

"Thanks. When I modeled, that's how my agent described my figure to clients."

"Yours are lovely, my dear. Laura and Angelica." Norman began caressing my right breast, which he called Laura. My mother's name.

I pushed his hand away.

Smiling mischievously, he put both hands back on the wheel. "Don't take offense. I'd like you to be in my movie. For the soundtrack would you let me tape your orgasms?"

"You must be joking." I glared at him. "Let me out of this car."

"Don't overreact. You need one of your meetings."

"Sure do, after that remark. Come with me?"

"Not this trip, but I like those meetings. They're good for characters. For my writing." Norman lowered his voice and chuckled. "Girls were fucking in the front row the last time."

"That's absurd!"

"That's what I saw. How could I find those meetings on my own?"

"I'll get you a meeting guide, but you can't speak unless you admit you're an alcoholic."

"I'm not an alcoholic." Norman turned up the jazz on the radio.

"I have the quiz in my handbag to find out if someone is. Want to take it?"

"Sure."

I read twenty questions that required a yes or a no. After much hesitation, he finished the quiz.

"Okay, Norman, you're an alcoholic."

"How's that? I drink because of my feelings. I need to drink. That's doesn't make me an alcoholic."

"I understand. I used to feel the same way. You have seven yes answers. More than three make you an alcoholic."

"Ask me the questions again," Norman said, pushing out his lower lip.

"You're not allowed a second chance, but I'll give you one because you've been a good sport." I gave him the quiz again, hoping that he would think about why he drank.

This time he had two yes answers.

"Norman, you cheated."

"The first time my concentration was off. I'm driving," he said. Norman's voice squeaked when he lied. He held the wheel with both hands.

"I want you to go to meetings for me if you won't go for you. You don't want to stop drinking because you think you're too old. That's not true. You're a periodic alcoholic."

"And you're a nag. I won't go at all."

Norman was quiet for a few minutes. "After I stabbed Adele, the doctors wanted me to go, but I wouldn't."

"You're so much nicer after meetings."

"So are you, but stop playing Carry Nation."

"I hate seeing your body being destroyed. You're puffed up from drinking, Norman. Bloated."

"That's the gout."

"That's alcohol destroying your liver. How do you manage to make love after you've been drinking?"

"If I've had too much to drink, I don't have sex."

"You prefer drinking to sex."

"That's not how I look at it. Drinking occurs first."

"You don't have enough control not to drink when you want to have sex?"

"You've made your point." Norman reached for my hand. His left hand remained on the wheel. "You wouldn't be happy with me. I'm irritable. Hard to live with. I get angry when dinner isn't on the table on time." He massaged my palm, looked at the road, and with resignation said, "Everyone likes Norris."

How difficult it must be to be Mailer's wife. I felt sad for everyone. How would this affair resolve itself? Norman and I couldn't live together. Our affair was working because we didn't live together. Living in the now became an excuse for not taking responsibility for the future.

Norman was sensitive to my silence. Sometimes I believed he could read my thoughts. "I want you to know I can fuck you even if you don't feel like it. You must tell me if you don't want to have sex. We don't have to every time we're together. We can just talk."

"I know that, Norman," I said, though I didn't know it at all.

"If you would come back to New York this fall, I'd see you two, three times a week if I didn't have a novel to write and the presidency of PEN. One day you'll get it into your thick head that I like you."

It was difficult for me to say no to Mailer. It would have been like rejecting Herbert, my father, and Norman, my love.

Sometimes I didn't feel like making love, but I was afraid I'd hurt Norman's feelings. I never wanted him to feel his sixty-two years of flesh bothered me when, in fact, it excited me. All that wisdom. Experience. I would rather have hurt myself than hurt Norman.

A fire engine passed us. Its sirens wailed.

"Norman, you know that peculiar, white-haired professor from the University of Pennsylvania who you introduced me to at Christmas? Why did you say he was one of the 'firemen'?"

"Bob Lucid happens to be my biographer and friend. You talk too much and ask too many questions," Norman said, his voice a growl. His expression contorted. "Try being quiet and enjoy the view."

What had happened to the tender, loving Norman that I had been talking to?

Norman's anger frightened me. While I was afraid of him and knew he was capable of doing things to harm me, physically, mentally, and economically, I accepted this fear as part of loving Norman who, like my father, had little control over his demons.

Still, I was being foolish to live in the now and not look to the future. How Norman had treated his ex-wives was an indication of how he would treat me when it ended. But I was so into my obsession with him that I was wearing blinders on my heart. I loved him and knew that to keep him in my life I could not put pressure on him. He needed a long leash, like a wild animal. Wild he was, and part of me loved the excitement so much that I made few demands on him. He would have a temper tantrum when confronted by my financial needs. In the beginning of our relationship, I learned to do without any support from him. I couldn't risk being thought of as a former wife pulling on him financially. After all, I wasn't a former wife. I was only his new lover.

On this trip, when Norman had said he wanted to turn me into an interviewer, I was flattered. I did not realize one of his chief reasons was for me to interview him to further his career and so that he could try to control each interview to protect his legacy. He demanded that he be able to edit his quotes. His image meant everything to him. For my last two interviews, I did not allow him to edit his text as he had wanted. After we broke up, his son John Buffalo, interviewed him and then his biographer, J. Michael Lennon. Norman could control both of these men just as he controlled his image for history. These men allowed Norman to edit his quotes, which was his way of hiding the truth. And while John Buffalo and J. Michael Lennon felt honored, they were also being manipulated, as was the public, by being presented with an inaccurate portrait of Norman Mailer.

At times I felt directed by Norman. He used his basso profondo voice and his anger to get his way. A childlike ploy. The bully.

I understood why Jean-Luc Godard had wanted Norman to star in Godard's version of *King Lear* in the summer of 1985. During our interview for *L.A. Magazine,* Norman told me he had agreed to star in *King Lear* on the condition that he be allowed to write and direct the film version of his novel, *Tough Guys Don't Dance*.

I tried to warn Norman about Godard.

Godard had filmed Jane Fonda, movie star, in the film *Tout va bien*. Simultaneously he was filming the documentary *Letter to Jane,* belittling Jane Fonda, anti-war activist, in Vietnam. Both films were shown together at the opening of the New York Film Festival in the presence of Jane Fonda, who had not known about the humiliating documentary.

Jean-Pierre Rassam, an old friend who produced these films, invited me to the festival and introduced me to Godard's assistant, Jean-Pierre Gorin. We began to date.

Through him, I learned a bit more about Godard. One night Gorin, whose passes I kept rejecting, told me he had cancer. He didn't know how long he had to live and wanted to make love to me. Though I felt sad for him, I rejected him once more. The next day I asked Rassam about Gorin's cancer and how long he had to live.

"He didn't try that on you?" Rassam laughed. "Sounds more like Godard."

Trying to save Norman from Godard's and Gorin's manipulation, I told Norman how Godard had tried to humiliate Jane Fonda.

Norman told me I was being paranoid.

In the summer of 1985 after rejecting two of Norman's scripts, Godard demanded a third rewrite. Begrudgingly, Norman complied.

Norman's daughter Kate, whose mother was Jeanne Campbell, was to play King Lear's daughter on film. Kate just had appeared off Broadway in *Uncle Vanya*. Then she was photographed for the cover of *Vanity Fair* because of her uncanny resemblance to Marilyn Monroe. For this cover a brunette Kate wore a blond wig and was made up to look like Marilyn.

Norman had given a copy of *Vanity Fair* to Godard, whose manipulative thoughts must have begun to brew.

In August, Norman and Kate began filming *King Lear* in St. Moritz. Godard did away with Norman's third rewrite and directed Kate and Norman to improvise. Norman realized that Godard was mocking him by trying to show an incestuous relationship between Norman and his daughter.

The Mailers walked and left Godard holding the camera. Proof of Godard's intentions was that though he had three scripts by Norman Mailer, he never made *King Lear* without Norman and Kate. Godard's deal to have Norman write the script had been a ploy to get Norman and Kate in front of his lens and under his manipulative direction.

Norman called me the day he returned from Switzerland. "You were right," he said.

"What happened?" I asked.

"I lost a pile of money and don't want to talk about it."

Norman's thick-skinned resilience was one of his finest qualities. He knew not to spread negativity, giving it power. Norman tried to hide his tyrannical nature and abusiveness by assuming his paternal image as much as possible. He had not fooled Jean-Luc Godard.

In 1986, at a fund-raising party for PEN at the Steinbergs', wealthy socialites more known for their greenmailing than their philanthropy, Norman introduced me to a modest Kate, who wore no makeup and underplayed her beauty and well-endowed sexuality, which had been revealed in the *Vanity Fair* photos. Norman had told me that I reminded him of Kate.

"Have you ever been sexually attracted to Kate?" I asked.

"No," he said. "But it's been close."

At the same party, hoping to make Norman jealous, I introduced him to Robin Williams, who had been a classmate in a comedy workshop. Robin, one of the hosts on Broadway for the PEN Congress, was about to film *Dead Poets Society* and was eager to meet Norman and the literary world. I enjoyed watching Robin study Norman for material while Norman studied Robin.

I did what Norman wanted out of fear. Off camera, Norman directed with his rage. I suspect Jean-Luc Godard knew this and wanted to direct Norman's rage on camera. What cinema verité it would be if Godard could show the angry child inside the literary enfant terrible by making Norman a victim of his own resentments on film.

As articulate as Norman was, when his intellect wasn't getting him what he wanted, he resorted to terrorizing tactics like a Mafia don. In 1989 *Vanity Fair* reported Norman's nickname was The Godfather.

I couldn't help thinking of Fanny Mailer's willingness to go to any length to please her son as being a force behind Norman's temper. Fanny withstood Barney Mailer's emotional abuse so that a thirteen-year-old Norman could have his way. She took the milk train to Boston so that her son could have freshly laundered shirts for his classes at Harvard.

"I felt smothered by my mother," Norman told me more than once.

Being directed by Norman's temper reminded me of being directed by Sam Peckinpah, who was notorious for his abuse of women.

Peckinpah directed me in *The Killer Elite*. When I auditioned for him, which was only more of a brief chat, I was surprised at his gentleness. He did not play the father figure like Norman did. Instead Peckinpah played the good boy/bad boy. When Peckinpah was good, he was very good, and when he was bad, he was brutal.

During our audition, Peckinpah stared at me for a long time without saying anything. I stared back at him. Silence was a manipulative ploy Peckinpah used to put others off guard so that they would become uncomfortable and reveal themselves.

Norman did not use silence to manipulate. He was too nervous to remain silent for any length of time. Peckinpah had a greater sense of calm, cool; therefore, when he revealed his rage by ranting and raving, his anger had a greater impact. Peckinpah was a peculiar man who reminded me of a sullen Scottish terrier with his scraggly white hair and whiskers and his dirty blue and white paisley kerchief that he tied around his forehead.

One hour after my audition, my agent told me I had the part. Some of my scenes were filmed in a hotel in Marina del Rey. At 6 a.m. when I arrived on the set, Peckinpah offered me breakfast—my choice of a vitamin B-12 shot, cocaine, marijuana, or an assortment of alcoholic beverages. I chose the B-12 shot.

At 9 a.m. James Caan, Robert Duvall, Burt Young, about ten actresses, and I were placed on the set. A debauched party scene. Peckinpah ordered the other actresses' clothing torn to reveal as much flesh as possible. He had chosen a blue suede dress for me and placed me closest to the camera.

When I was alone with Peckinpah, he was soft-spoken. On the set he became the shrill martinet. He instructed makeup to be applied as though we, the women, were sluts.

As he stared at me I thought, "If you put that makeup on me, I'll walk."

"Leave her alone," he said sotto voce to makeup.

Before he shouted "Action!" amyl nitrate was popped under the other actresses' nostrils while he directed them to further expose themselves.

Again Peckinpah left me alone.

After the party scene, an actress, whom Peckinpah had directed to reveal her enormous breasts on camera, was taken to a room with members of the crew and Peckinpah. She had been plied with alcohol and drugs. She had wanted to please her director.

As I listened to her sexual groans through the door marked "Closed Set," I felt angry and yet sad for everyone.

The next day, while wearing a bikini bottom, I filmed a bedroom scene with James Caan. After Peckinpah explained the situation, he said, "Now improvise." The crew leered and laughed at Caan's quips and at what I thought was the awkwardness of our trying to relate to each other.

When I saw the movie, my scene with James Caan was missing. There had never been film in the camera.

Like Norman, Peckinpah was an alcoholic. While drunk, he dove into the pool of the Beverly Hilton. There was no water in it. He survived. He stopped drinking. Eventually.

Norman, unlike Peckinpah, was a gentle director.

For the filming of *Tough Guys Don't Dance*, *New Woman* flew me to Provincetown to interview Isabella Rossellini. While there, I was offered an assignment from *Us Magazine* to interview Norman. As I watched him calmly direct a scene, he seemed more concerned with the actors' opinions of him as a director rather than his opinion of their acting.

On my last day I crashed a "closed" bedroom set. Here, a fatherly Norman Mailer directed an apparently naked and beautiful Debra Sandlund, who was being made love to by Ryan O'Neal. Did Norman have film in his camera? Was he abusing a young, innocent actress as I had been abused by Peckinpah? Was I watching the filming of *Tough Guys Don't Dance* or *Deer Park*?

Norman spotted me and belligerently ordered me off the set. We went to his trailer and had it out. I never did find out if Norman had film in his camera, but the scene was not in the movie.

While Peckinpah was the better director, Mailer was the better actor, but Godard was the most manipulative.

Norman even acted when he drove. With his chin raised, his hands evenly holding the wheel, and his forced serenity, he could have been a limousine driver. After his outburst I stopped talking to him.

Why did the mention of "the firemen" upset him so? Now I was more curious. Another secret. Norman's sexual appetite was insatiable and had no bounds.

While Norman had the car on cruise control, my imagination had been on overdrive. Why not enjoy the moment? It was a glorious summer day, and Norman and I were going to have a loving few hours alone in a new environment, free of memories.

I rolled my window down and inhaled the scent of pine.

"Roll that window up a little, please," Norman said. "I'm sorry if I was abrupt, but I don't want anything to ruin this day." He held my hand and studied my expression.

"You have so many secrets, Norman."

"I do. I have so many wives and children, secrets are a part of it. Please don't pry. You remind me of a nagging wife. When we're together, I don't want to be reminded of the pressures of marriage."

Norman's explanation made sense. I would try not to be demanding. Because he had six wives, I had to be careful not to act like a seventh, but I wanted to know who "the firemen" were. Probably a group of his friends who put out sexual fires by introducing each other to women. Orgy cronies. The only orgy I'd been in was in the movie *Looking for Mr. Goodbar* and that was simply hard work. The concept of an orgy seemed like mass victimization. I knew they had been only a sport to Norman.

During the PEN Congress in 1986, Norman arranged for me to spend a lot of time with Bob Lucid. I grew to admire Lucid's gentle nature and smooth way of dealing with people. Norman had instructed Lucid to watch my movies. "Baby Snooks," Norman would call me, still leaving notes in my father's name. The curiosity that Norman encouraged in my writing, he discouraged in my life.

In honor of the PEN Congress, the Canadian Embassy threw a party where I was introduced to Pierre Trudeau. Within minutes of shaking my hand, he invited me to lunch. He showed no restraint, no fear of public opinion, yet I remembered reading that his image meant a great deal to him. I was flattered by his bold flirtation.

Over lunch at the Russian Tea Room, Trudeau told me, "The PEN Congress is so chaotic that I haven't met its president. Norman Mailer and I don't seem to be in the same place at the same time."

Later I told Norman, "You know, Pierre Trudeau would like to meet you. Do you want me to arrange it?"

"Of course!" Norman said.

The meeting was scheduled for the coffee shop of the St. Moritz Hotel. Norman's biographer, Bob Lucid, showed up instead. Lucid said Norman had a pressing commitment. Instead of introducing Norman to Trudeau, Norman had put me in the position of introducing Lucid to Trudeau. The next day, Lucid introduced Norman to Trudeau when I was not present.

Over the years there would be many things I would do for Norman that would go unnoticed. One way I found to defend myself against Norman's manipulation was to let him think that he was in control.

One night after a PEN dinner at the St. Moritz, I stayed late with Norman. Lucid seemed to be directing what appeared to be a series of slamming of doors in various suites. In these suites there were close male and female friends of Norman's. I wondered if Lucid was a "fireman," arranging late-night sexual encounters in the hotel for his good friend Norman on PEN's budget.

"Turn it off," I told myself. When would we arrive? This drive was endless. We had been on congested freeways, through claustrophobic tunnels filled with carbon monoxide fumes, over winding mountain roads where we had to stop for a herd of sheep crossing our path. Bugs attacked the windshield. At last we were coming to the sea. The two-lane highway needed resurfacing. I held my stomach.

"Norman, can you drive a bit slower? I'm getting carsick."

"Sorry, my pet, I thought you'd prefer this route."

"I'm nauseous. Could we stop at that McDonald's? I need a coke."

"Could you hold on a bit longer? We're almost there."

"I'll try, Norman," I said, longing for a Big Mac. Enough of Norman's fantasy. This had to be an incredible home. Northern California architecture. Frank Lloyd Wright maybe? An ivy-covered mansion with a circular driveway, surrounded by wrought iron fences and gates. I began to fantasize about the palatial splendor of this magnificent home on a lake belonging to Norman's good friend. I never knew whom I was going to meet with Norman, and most often it was a pleasant surprise.

After three hours of driving, I was hungry and tired. "When are we getting there?" I asked Norman as we drove through a suburban village. He stopped to consult his map. His friend had written detailed directions. Norman would not tell me the name of his friend. I gazed at the homes we were passing and thought, "How awful! Wood frame, two stories, one-car garages, suburban prefab housing."

"It's up the street," Norman said. "We're here!" He smiled as we pulled into a dirty driveway barely missing a tricycle. No one was home. I didn't know who'd want to be. It was a drab grey house like the others on the block, but this was more run-down than the rest.

I was starved.

Norman found the key in the mailbox and grinned as though it were a hidden treasure. The door creaked as he opened it. Roaches scurried. Cobwebs hung around its edges.

I had hoped to be greeted by a waiter holding a tray of caviar. "I don't like this house," I said, brushing a spider off my forearm.

"Now, now. We can make love outside in the backyard and look at the bay at the same time. No one will see us." Norman's eyes grew wide.

My stomach growled. Why did we drive three hours to make love in this filthy place when we had a luxurious suite at the St. Francis back in the city—with excellent room service and at no cost to Norman?

"This is crazy, Norman." I walked into the living room, furnished with an old sofa covered in dust, a broken TV, and a fireplace in need of cleaning. "I want to leave."

"Come onto the terrace," he said, determined to persuade me of the sexual charms of this run-down ghost house.

I followed Norman onto the back patio. A barbecue showed some signs of life as well as a few empty beer cans that had been strewn about.

"Look at the bay," Norman said with his legs spread, hands on hips.

"What about it?" I said as I watched the sun setting on the water then glanced behind me. A rusty screen was about to fall out of the second-story window.

"Norman, why did you bring me here?"

"Come on. Please an old man with your charms. This is a special moment for me." Norman pulled me close to him.

"This is not my thing."

"Well, do an acting improvisation. You can pretend we're in Monte Carlo."

"I don't like Monte Carlo, and I don't like this house." Norman kissed me.

I froze.

"Why can't you please me?" Norman said in an imploring tone.

"I'm always pleasing you, but this filthy pigsty is disgusting."

"Don't you want to be in my movie? I need to see that you can use your mind to create a scene of sensuality." Norman ran his hand between my legs.

I pushed his hand away. "Don't pull that one. Why did you bring me here? If you were honest with me, maybe I could have some honest feelings."

Norman dodged my question, dropped his pants, and sat on the brick wall covered in dirt. "Ouch!" He grimaced. "What did I sit on?"

"Let me see? Turn around and bend over." For a moment Norman was my docile patient. He wanted to be taken care of, to be mothered. As I pulled thorns out of his buttocks, I noticed Norman developing an erection.

"Forget about the thorns. You've gotten most of them. Being here with you excites me."

"I don't understand your erection, Norman."

"I used to come here long ago. It has memories," he said, massaging himself.

"If you share them with me, maybe this house will mean something to me too."

"It's nothing to speak about. I want to make love to you here. Now. Don't ask why."

"No, Norman, I want to get out of here. You are being perverse."

Norman hesitated, then realized he couldn't control me.

As we drove away from the dilapidated ghost house, I wondered why it held such a fascination for Norman. It smelled. Dust and dirt covered everything. Was he trying to act out a scene in a novel he wanted to write?

"Norman, did you bring me here for research for your novel?"

"Of course not."

"This day has been a complete waste of time!"

"You don't like my company?" Norman said, pushing his chin in the air.

I realized I had gone too far. Something about this creepy house had special meaning to Norman, and if I pushed him, he felt controlled. I would become another nagging wife. I couldn't allow that. No, I would have to overlook his mysterious obsession and focus on my own with Mailer and why I was putting up with this crap.

On our ride back to the hotel we stopped at a restaurant on the coast and ate barbecued oysters on a patio overlooking the sea. The sun was setting on the water and seagulls flew by us. I excused myself to go to the ladies' room and washed my hands more than once. Why was I in love with this madman? I thought about my father trying to antagonize my mother by driving into that nudist colony. Once more Norman reminded me of my father. But my father wasn't a sexual deviant. Was Mailer? It certainly was in his literature. He must like to act out scenes before he writes them, I thought. Did Anaïs Nin go through this with Henry Miller? Please. Maybe my attraction to Norman was in my head and was going to stay there. Who was he to treat me like a cheap hooker and waste my day on this tawdry fantasy? Just another dirty old man, I thought, as I walked back to the table.

"Sorry the day wasn't what I had hoped it would be," Norman said. "Look, this is past the peak of my life. The end. I used to be a great fuck. Today I'm not. I'm trying to cope. Boy, I'm glad I didn't know you then."

"Why do you talk this way? You think your entire worth is in your sexuality. Why do you think so little of yourself?" I said without realizing that I could have been talking to myself.

"My mother used to say that to me."

"You place too much importance on sex."

"Twelve years ago you wouldn't have married me."

"What does that mean?"

Norman gazed at the sun setting on the ocean.

"Norman, let's go back to the hotel. I want to get those thorns out of you. Maybe we can take a bath together."

"We can't both fit into the tub."

"We can try."

I was grateful to return to the St. Francis where I stayed in the tub for one hour and vowed, "No more side trips with Norman Mailer."

That night I fell asleep with my toes touching Norman's. I had difficulty staying asleep. I kept wondering what had been done to Norman to make him so afraid to reveal his feelings? Why did he feel he had to prove his sexuality? Then I wondered why I had to prove my own sexuality? Insecurity. But his mother had nurtured him while mine had been critical. Finally I fell off into a deep, much needed slumber.

The next morning Norman awakened first. "You want breakfast outside the hotel? Wake up!" he said, ready to march.

After walking about a mile up and down hills in search of a restaurant, I said, "Oh, Norman, let's go anywhere."

"No, I know there's a nice café at the top of the next hill," Norman said, repeating himself. "Ah, there it is!" He stood legs spread, hands on hips and pointed.

"Great!" I said covered in perspiration.

Norman pushed open the door of a quaint coffeehouse filled with young people reading books and newspapers. No wonder Norman had wanted to find this restaurant. He began reading the front page of the *New York Times* while I grabbed the Entertainment section. Peering up from the paper, Norman said, "Tonight I'd like to have dinner with Tom Luddy, who's producing my movie, and Spalding Gray. You're perfect for the role of Madeleine in *Tough Guys*."

"How'd you meet him?"

"Produces for Coppola. Francis introduced us."

"I like Francis."

"You know him?"

"He came to my hotel for brunch when I tested for *The Fan Club*."

"He came to you? How'd you do that?"

"For someone who hates questions, you ask a lot of them. Coppola and I were introduced by a journalist, Marie Brenner, when I was engaged to Claude Picasso."

"So Claude was a friend of Coppola's?"

"No, Claude's ex-wife was. Coppola and Claude had a prickly friendship."

"Prickly?"

"In the early seventies when Coppola met Claude, he told Claude that if his mother won her lawsuit against the French government, and Claude was awarded Picasso's millions, he should give his money away. 'Too much money is a bad thing,' Coppola said."

"How did Claude react?"

"He didn't like it. We thought Coppola was bragging, but he later went bankrupt after investing his own money in his own projects."

"That doesn't explain why Coppola came to you for brunch."

"Norman, it's difficult knowing when you're being jealous or caring."

"It's important for me to understand your relationship. Coppola and I are doing business," Norman said.

"We are friends," I said, spilling too much syrup on my pancakes. "You're not the only person who has the right to do business with him."

"Don't be defensive. Just answer my question."

"In '75, when I left Claude, Columbia flew me to Hollywood to test for *The Fan Club*. I called Coppola when I arrived at the Beverly Hills Hotel. He already knew that I was testing."

"He took your call?"

"Sure. Those tests were the talk of Hollywood. Racquel Welch, Sophia Loren, and Brigitte Bardot were offered the part but didn't like the script. Fifteen hundred actresses across America auditioned."

"Who else tested?"

"Lynda Carter, Marjorie Wallace, who had been a Miss World, Catherine Bach. Why?"

Norman cleared his throat. "I'm looking for actresses to test for my film. Who produced and directed *The Fan Club*?"

"Peter Guber and Larry Gordon produced and Nic Roeg directed."

"Who got the part?"

"The film was never made."

Norman coughed while swallowing. "Why?"

"Columbia couldn't get James Poe to write an acceptable script."

"Sounds like someone was ripping off Columbia." Norman finished his coffee. "Be on your good behavior tonight with Luddy."

"What's that supposed to mean?"

"Don't talk too much and don't ask questions."

"Maybe you should call an escort service."

"Don't start. Luddy is business for both of us. I'm trying to help you."

That night, Spalding Gray and Tom Luddy fussed over Norman, who reciprocated. I stared at the white walls, tried to listen, tried not to ask questions and yet feel a part of the evening. Norman drank a lot. Scotch.

After dinner Norman and I visited the bookshop, City Lights. He bought me paperbacks of Chandler, DeLillo, and Barthelme.

"Study Chandler for his scenes and short sentences. You can learn a great deal from him."

When I saw a copy of *Double Indemnity*, I asked, "Could I have this?"

"Buy it if you want it."

I did. I loved going to bookstores with Norman, especially in San Francisco. People were respectful of Norman's feelings and rarely acknowledged his presence. A furtive admiration. Literary. Loving.

Afterwards, Norman led me to the more depressing part of the city. As we turned a corner, a billboard with a photo of an almost topless Carol "Do Do" Cheng towered above us. Bouncers stood by roped-off entrances to strip clubs.

"I like a good go-go club," Norman said, studying photos of half-naked women under glass outside one of the establishments. "Once I gave a black girl five dollars after she stripped."

I wondered why Norman was bragging about being cheap.

He began counting bills to give to a bouncer, who glared down at Norman, dismissing him as another horny geriatric. The reverence of the people in the bookshop seemed to have been for another person.

"Norman, this is not my idea of a good time."

"That Pennsylvania Dutch side of you is not your most creative. One day I want to take you to a club in Kansas City and have you strip. That would please me."

"Norman, don't disgust me."

"You're such a Puritan. I want to share you."

"What I do when we're alone I do because I love you. I am not a stripper."

"That's how Jerry Hall got Mick Jagger.'

"Then go fuck Jerry Hall!" Clutching Chandler, De Lillo, Barthelme, and James M. Cain, I turned, hailed a cab, and stepped into it.

Back at the hotel I took a hot bath, put a green masque on my face, then crawled into bed and began to read *Double Indemnity*.

How can Norman teach me to write when we have such different beliefs? He believed in alcohol and that getting drunk was fun. I believed in sobriety. He believed in abusing women. I believed in nurturing men and women as I was trying to do with Norman. He believed in chaos. I believed in serenity. I wanted him to edit my work, but would he edit my point of view? Marriage wasn't his biggest problem. Norman Mailer didn't respect women. Would he ever understand me? Or did he only care about his own stimulation?

He'd been drinking. That was a separate problem.

We didn't view sex the same way, though we liked to write about it, and he liked to read my work. I worshipped D.H. Lawrence; Norman was a devotee of Henry Miller.

I heard a key in the door.

Norman's face was flushed.

I thought of my father returning from what mother called a "dirty movie." I thought about how happy we were to have him safe at home. I remembered how he would be covered in perspiration and wild with stimulation, as Norman was now.

"Don't ever leave me again," he said, sitting on the bed. "You know I was kidding."

"Oh, Norman, this morning you wanted to tape my orgasm. Tonight you want me to be a stripper. I think you've confused me with an object."

"Only on Fridays. It's Thursday. I want you."

"Very funny. I won't make love to you when you've been drinking."

"Then fuck me." Norman grinned, wiping the sweat from his brow.

"Exactly what I won't do."

"I've only had scotch. With water, I might add," Norman said, holding me.

"Three too many," I said, pulling away from his grasp. Then I rolled over and closed my eyes.

"Have it your way," Norman said.

A shudder went through me. I remembered my father saying that to my mother when he'd lost a fight. When she'd refused to have sex with him.

I thought about the men I'd had sex with when I had been drugged or drunk. How I'd felt. Like a machine. On automatic pilot. Feelings neutralized. Anesthetized. Alcohol made sex safe. No one cared. Next day—who was that? Didn't matter if I'd stood on my head, naked, or had sex on top of a Cadillac under the moonlight. If I'd been drunk, sex had been performance. The man, a receptacle. So was I. Gymnasiums of flesh to relieve tension. Sex was for loneliness, not love. Insecurity, not conviction. I loved Norman Mailer and refused to fuck him or to allow him to fuck me.

During the night Norman took a pill.

In the morning he awakened me with a kiss. Dr. Jekyll had returned. "Thank you for not making love to me last night."

"If you want to drink, drink, but I won't make love to you. What's that pill you took?"

"Spying on me, are ya?" Norman grinned.

"What's it for?"

"My heart."

"Good God!"

"Doctors wanted to operate, but I wouldn't let them."

"Norman, you've got to look at your drinking. Alcohol's bad for your heart."

"It's good in moderation."

"Last night wasn't moderation."

Norman held me. "I drank because of my feelings. I have to direct soon. Luddy's my producer. When I'm alone with you, I don't feel like drinking."

"Oh, Norman, I used to feel like that. If you'd just come to meetings..."

"Don't preach. Focus on your own life."

Norman was right. By focusing on him, I didn't have to look at what was happening to me. I was making Norman the center of my world, and I was living on a fault line. He was a married man whose commitment to me was "talk." He had said he would arrange for me to have a life insurance policy, but his agent Scott Meredith had to do this. Scott Meredith stalled year after year about making arrangements to protect me in my twilight years.

But I told myself, after all, I had been a model. Being beautiful had been how I earned my living. I didn't expect to be beautiful for the rest of my life. My looks had gotten me in trouble with men. When they faded, it might be a relief.

People would have to deal with me in other ways. Accept me on other terms. Aging, I hoped, could be liberating. So why think about it now when Norman was in love with me? And because he liked to make love to me, maybe he would want to get sober.

I believed Norman would die if he didn't get help. His body was puffed up. Gout, he called it. Bad liver, it was. And what about his kidneys? Every time he went to a party he drank. The next day he was hungover and had trouble getting into his writing. Could he think logically with a hangover? Would his plot be chaotic? He was so skilled technically that he could craft a well-structured sentence drunk or sober, but would he be in control of his story?

Becoming sober didn't mean only giving up alcohol, it meant coming to terms with his childhood, which, if left unresolved, became reason to drink.

No doubt *The Executioner's Song* and *The Armies of the Night* were great books Norman had written when he was obvious about his drinking, but when I met him in 1983, Norman just had written *Tough Guys Don't Dance*, a convoluted tale about decapitating women. Was Norman's anger toward women dominating his muse?

"Once I sat on an actress's head and held her cunt open to the camera," Norman told me with pride. Norman bragged about sitting on a woman's head and felt that it was a creative thought to cut off a woman's head. He was preoccupied with silencing women. Changing a woman's identity was a form of silencing a woman. In the Manso biography, Midge Decter said, "Norman invents a lady character, then marries someone who has to play this roll."

Now I wanted him to turn me into a writer. To educate me with his genius. To mold me. Why wasn't I seeing the signals? The danger? While he could teach me the craft of writing, did I want him to impose his beliefs on my work? He believed in drinking and in abusing women. Until Norman resolved his anger toward his mother, he would continue to abuse women. Alcohol and the thinking that accompanied drinking enabled this abuse.

If I knew so much, why couldn't I extricate myself? I wanted him to fix me, to rescue me as I tried to rescue him. I wanted Norman to create a new sober me, no longer remembered as Hollywood's beanbag for abuse. I wanted Norman's genius to give me respect when, in fact, I was giving his genius the power to abuse me.

Though Norman's ego was gargantuan, his self-respect was as low as mine. "You only know one quarter of me," he would say. "You don't know how bad I am."

I knew how bad he was. Norman Mailer was an alcoholic filled with self-loathing. Just like me.

Norman and I lay in each other's arms. I pulled away and looked into his eyes. Pus had gathered in the corners. His red veins were prominent. Though we just had awakened, he appeared tired. "Thanks, Norman," I said, wishing I could focus on my life. "I'll try not to nag, but don't ask my permission to drink."

"I didn't last night," Norman said wide-eyed.

"You do sometimes."

"That's to show respect."

"Puts me in a position of control. Mothering that you want, then resent. A set up. A con. You have to do what you want to do."

"I don't believe I'm hearing this."

"It doesn't matter that you're in a marriage that you can't get out of. It matters if you're dead. Your drinking is killing you."

"Knew you'd buy it back." Norman shook his head and stared at the ceiling.

"If your drinking gets in the way of our relationship, I'll just stop seeing you."

"Listen to you."

"You won't. That's the point."

"Look, I've never been to meetings for alcoholics with anyone else. Let me do it my way."

"I love you, Norman."

Norman held me as we sat on the bed gazing at the floor. I felt safe. At peace.

Still, I wanted to change Norman. My trying to change him was dangerous, not only if I wanted to help him, but also if I wanted him to love me. But especially because I wasn't concentrating on myself.

Chapter 14

Though the morning light had filtered through the lace draperies of the St. Francis Hotel, I had gone back to sleep in Norman's arms. When he released me from his embrace, he cocked his head. "You drifted off into oblivion, my sweet." He paused. "Has anyone told you that you look like Linda Darnell?"

"You. When I was that fruit salad on top of the table in New York."

"Ah! I remember. Senior moment. How could I have forgotten that 'feast de resistance'?"

I poked him in his tummy for his bad pun. "How many people have told you that you look like Spencer Tracy?"

"No one but you." Norman squeezed my thigh. "Now would you like to do some sightseeing?"

"Where shall we go?"

"Let's walk to the Top of the Mark, get a map, then go to Coit Tower."

I put on my marching shoes.

At Coit Tower, two men asked for Norman's autograph, which flattered him. We walked around the promenade, put coins into the telescopes to look at the view of the Golden Gate, then decided to go to Chinatown for lunch.

Walking downhill was refreshing. After mulling over the many restaurants, Norman chose one on a second story with a view of the congested alley. Plastic beads hung in the entrance. The walls were a Dayglo green. We were the only couple. After we began eating, we found out why.

We discussed the Peter Manso book on Mailer, just published. Though Norman had fought with Manso, Norman had bought me the book. Norman liked to see his name in print. In New York he bought each of the daily papers, read the gossip columns, and valued his relationship with columnists.

"That Manso book made me aware of my mortality."

"Also your Fiorinals."

"Never mind about them." Norman spilled lo mein on his sweater.

"Why did you grab your chest the last time you had an orgasm?"

"Have you read the entire Manso book?"

"Changing the conversation is my trick," I said. "Okay. Why don't you admit that you met Marilyn Monroe? Shelley Winters is convincing when she claims that you did."

"That's just Shelley being Shelley. I had a thing with her a long time ago in Hollywood."

"During *The Naked and the Dead*?"

"About then. We spent a good deal of time together. Every morning before she went to the studio, she would give blowjobs to Burt Lancaster. Then when I would see her, she would be in curlers looking a wreck."

"Did you ever let her know how you felt?"

"Years later she wanted me. But she had had her opportunity. She had been in love with Burt."

Norman's response reminded me of his need to control a woman. Shelley Winters had offended Norman's ego. He would never forgive her.

Norman added soy sauce to his lo mein. "This lobster has no taste."

"Neither does this restaurant."

"Touché. I want to talk to you about your writing. How much Chandler have you read?"

"*The Long Goodbye* and *Farewell, My Lovely*. I'm trying to get *Playback*."

"Not his best. Read a few pages of Chandler before you write. He's more the feel of your novel than O'Hara."

"You said in interviews that you don't read when you're writing. You said, 'If you're at work on your car and all the pieces are on the garage floor, you don't feel good if a Ferrari zooms by.'"

"Memorizing my quotes, are ya?" Norman grinned. He pushed up the sleeves of his navy V-neck sweater. I noticed the usual holes at the elbows. "Don't do as I do, do as I say. You have a tendency to be afraid to break up your dialogue with prose."

"Don't know how to."

"Study Chandler. Learn."

"I'm feeling you're holding a whip over my hand about using short sentences."

"Use a long one from time to time to give impact to the short."

"But you tell me I can't handle long sentences."

"Learn. The brain's a muscle. The more you write, the stronger it will become."

"I'm taking Basic Writing at U.C.L.A. I'm regressing. From Creative Writing to Basic Writing."

"That's ego."

"Yes, boss," I said, crumbling a fortune cookie.

"Pay attention." Norman leaned forward, placing his forearms on the table. "Before you write, read the section you last wrote. This will give the same tone and feel to your work. Make your own choices."

"I do that. That's when I edit. Well, try to edit."

"You must edit your own work. Make your own choices."

"I can't edit my work like you do."

"Give it time," Norman said, pouring tea. "You can't write mediocrity."

"Some days I feel like giving up. Too much to learn."

"I wrote *Of a Fire on the Moon* when I was going through a divorce. That's when I knew I was a writer. Now, let's walk to Fisherman's Wharf."

About 3 p.m. we were tired of watching the catamarans. Norman had another idea. "Want to go to a movie? *Silverado*?"

"Kevin Costner?"

"Right."

"Let's go."

We waited for a taxi that never came so we took a bus. Norman had a map, but he knew San Francisco. After entering the small theater, Norman bought popcorn and sodas. We sat in the middle of the movie house awaiting a real treat. Reviews on *Silverado* had been excellent. After half an hour, Norman and I looked at each other and left.

"Terrible," Norman said.

"Maybe it gets better, but why wait?"

Norman got on the first bus we saw. After a few minutes I said, "Norman, this bus is going the wrong way."

"What makes you say that?"

"We're going back to Fisherman's Wharf! We want to go uphill, not around."

"You might be right," Norman said as he consulted the crumpled map shoved into his frayed pants pocket.

We reached the hotel two hours later. And I had vowed no more side trips with Norman Mailer.

That night before dinner, Norman rearranged the furniture so that a chair was in front of the mirrored armoire. He wanted to play "casting couch."

He came out of the bathroom wearing only a sailor's hat he had bought at Fisherman's Wharf. He yanked at his favorite self and said, "Now walk into the room as though I'm the director, and you're auditioning for the role of a sex symbol who's been raped and is afraid to go to the police because of bad publicity."

I went outside the room and knocked on the door.

"Yes," Norman said. "Come in."

Wide-eyed I walked in and stood in front of him.

"Who have we here?" Norman said, pulling at himself.

"I'm Estelle Meriweather from the Perkins Agency. Here for the reading, Mr. Mailer."

"Well, Miss Meriweather, what a lovely face and body you have. Do you mind sitting in this chair in front of the armoire so that I can look at you for various camera angles?"

"No, not at all, Mr. Mailer."

"And take off that outfit. I need to see your bone structure. Very important for the scenes with our heroine."

I stood there naked, about to take off my stockings, garter belt, and heels.

"No, no, Miss Meriweather. Leave them on. They show defiance."

I began to think Norman was nuts, but played along with him to humor him and sat in the chair. I didn't like this game. It was too real. It reminded me of my test for *The Fan Club*. Norman had the language and manipulation down pat. Too pat.

"Now can you recite some dialogue for me?"

"Yes, Mr. Mailer, what dialogue?" I asked myself where I got the stamina for these shenanigans.

"I vant to be a star and will do anything necessary to get this part," Norman said in his basso profondo voice.

"Norman, this is silly. I don't want to do this," I said into the mirror facing me. I stared at Norman's reflection.

He held me from behind and ran his hands over my body. Once the game ended, and I felt Norman's touch and smelled his scent, my true feelings surfaced and the third eye that had been watching him in disbelief disappeared. Why did he need this infantile role playing? More importantly, why was I putting up with it? Finally I had taken a stand, and it felt good.

After we made love, I gave him a much-needed manicure. "Why don't you take care of your nails?" I said, looking at his cuticles that had been bitten. "Your hands are tools. God's given you a gift, and you're abusing it. Your nails belong to a mechanic."

"Norris cuts hair. She doesn't do nails," Norman said, chuckling.

"I'd rather have your hands than your hair," I said, filing away. After I finished, I took a nice hot bath, then began to dress.

When I came out of the bathroom, Norman was seated on the bed. "Why am I always waiting for women?" he asked.

"You don't seem disturbed by it," I said, sitting by his side.

"I feel good." Norman reached for my hand and looked into my eyes. "Maybe it's because of the wonderful days we've spent together. I want you to meet me in Cape Cod in August."

Another invitation. Another trip across America. I was beginning to feel as though my affair with Norman was like performing a literary shuttle service. Still, I was flattered and would look forward to another trip to be by his side. Even if it felt a bit manipulative. I wasn't ready to get off the merry-go-round of denial with The Great One.

Chapter 15

In November of 1985, I sublet my apartment in Hollywood to be with Norman in New York. He found us a tiny one-bedroom on the fourth floor of a brownstone on East 62nd Street in Manhattan. The PEN Celebration was about to begin. Norman, who was the President of PEN, wanted me to attend and to be close to him. I felt he loved me because he wanted me by his side at this important time for him. Though moving my possessions from one side of the United States to the other was a feat, I felt it was worth it to be with Norman. He had become the center of my life. When we were apart, I was sad and sat by the phone instead of by him. I still went to my meetings with recovering alcoholics, but my heart belonged to Mailer.

Sometimes if Norman were deep into his writing, I would meet him in Brooklyn Heights. My writing lesson would be in his studio, a few brownstones from the duplex where his family lived.

Norman and I would rendezvous at his favorite Italian restaurant, Queen, on Court Street. He even invited my mother to lunch with us on occasion. They were friends. The maitre d' of Queen would fuss over Norman, who could be irritable when he was writing. We would share a pasta and then a veal dish. Rarely would he drink alcohol around me.

After lunch, Norman and I would stroll through the charming tree-lined streets of Brooklyn Heights and along the promenade. He never worried about being seen by his family or by his neighbors.

Then we would climb four flights to his studio. I would be exhausted. Norman would be rejuvenated.

"Good exercise for the knees," he would say. "I'm fighting the gout."

"It's your drinking," I would say while I, "the teetotaler," would huff and puff.

The studio's main room had a breathtaking view of Manhattan and the Brooklyn Bridge. In a tiny room off to the side, there was a single bed. Brightly colored designer sheets covered the mattress.

"I like these sheets," I said one day. "Who changes them?"

"The maid."

The studio was sloppy, sometimes downright dirty. Never the sheets. In the Pullman kitchen, stained coffee cups sat in the sink. The floors weren't swept. One wall was covered with bookshelves while books, mostly by Mailer, were stacked on the floor. A table with two captain's chairs sat in front of the big bay window. Norman's manuscripts, yellow legal pads, an electric pencil sharpener, and a stack of #2 pencils were arranged neatly on the table. Norman was organized with his writing.

In the center of the studio there was an exercise machine. A gravity machine. Perhaps ten feet high and three feet wide. It was designed for someone to step onto a small platform and to secure buckles around his waist and his feet. By pressing a button, the entire contraption turned upside down like an hourglass.

"What's this for?" I said.

"My circulation. I told you about it when we first met. If I write too long, I become tired. I strap myself into this, turn myself upside down for a spell and blood and oxygen rush back into my brain." Norman's eyes grew wide.

"I want you to take off all of your clothes, and I'll strap you into this."

"Norman, are you crazy?"

"Leave your heels on," he said, knowing I usually did what he wanted.

Giving pleasure to Norman and pleasing him were important to me. I wanted him to love me until I fell out of love with him, but my feelings were so intense that I couldn't imagine this happening. I loved Norman one minute at a time and was grateful for each moment—even if this meant that I had to be strapped naked onto some goddamn machine and turned upside down like a fruitcake.

As I stared at the ceiling with my head inches from the floor, Norman began to go down on me. He was humming and sounded a bit like a blender stuck on low.

I stared at his shoelaces, wondering why one was untied.

He held my knees apart and continued sighing passionately while I studied his sneakers. He was old and could trip one day, all because he hadn't tied his shoelaces.

Norman continued his lovemaking.

I couldn't see his eyes. Only his sneakers.

He was mesmerized, in a trance. Did he do this to Norris before or after a party?

What did I know? It was all I could do to keep from throwing up.

I faked a few sighs, which I rarely did to gratify Norman's need to prove his virility. But I was getting tired of playing "casting couch" and now this. How long could I continue to coddle Norman's infantile sexual urges? Then suddenly I said, "Norman, I feel sick."

"Oh, my dear, you don't like this?" Norman said gallantly while looking down at me.

"It's not you. It's the machine. I want to look at you, not your sneakers."

"Okay, okay. I just wanted to try it," Norman said good naturedly, like a child who'd been caught with both hands in the cookie jar.

Norman swung me right-side up. I ran into the bedroom. "I need to lie down," I said as I crawled under the sheets.

"You're not in a creative mood today, my darling."

"Norman, I don't like gadgets, contraptions, casting couch fantasies, old run-down houses in the middle of nowhere. I don't want to make love to an idea, a location, or a fantasy. I want to make love to you."

"Well, my pet, we won't do that again. It feels good to be wanted."

He crawled under the covers and held me. I wondered if Norman's pleasure had been to dominate me? Had he really dominated me if I had allowed him to do it? Was Norman testing me?

I looked up from the bed at what appeared to be a phone booth painted in dark colors. Photos covered with graffiti were shellacked here and there.

"What's that?" I said.

"That's the orgone box that I told you about. After I stabbed Adele, the doctors said I had to go in there and scream and pound the walls to get rid of my anger."

"Did you?"

"Scream and pound the walls? I did."

"And your anger?"

"My dear, it's still with me, but not to the same extent."

"Does writing help you to get it out?"

"Of course. So does sex."

And Norman let me make love to him.

Chapter 16

In the fall of 1985, a friend of mine, who was an editor at *Elle* magazine, wanted me to interview Norman talking about his upcoming presidency of PEN's 48th International Congress. It was to be held in New York in January of 1986.

Norman agreed, then taught me how to do an interview. "Divide your questions into subjects," he said. "Categories such as childhood, career, current events, sex, and relationships. Double tape record in case something goes wrong with one cassette."

While interviewing Norman, I learned to use an old acting trick. I imagined I was talking to a baby. This "as if" exercise softened my voice, forced me to speak slowly, and helped Norman to relax and to feel safe.

When asking questions about Norman's childhood, because of his drinking problem, I asked questions that I once had to ask myself in order to stay sober. Once I stopped drinking, I had to look at why I drank. I learned to ask my subjects some of these same questions.

And so my career as a journalist began.

In the beginning, our interviews were fun, mental gymnastics, verbal fencing. With each interview, I learned a bit more about Norman and his secrets. I became less concerned with his approval. Gradually, over the years, while doing nine interviews with him, his bullying attempts to control turned my feelings of challenge into defiance. Norman laughed less and became suspect of my line of questioning. In retrospect, our interviews turned into a bloody nine rounds.

But in the beginning, interviewing Norman was fun and exciting. He loved publicity, and I thought it was kind of him to trust me with this responsibility.

A few days after I had transcribed the first interview, he came to my apartment to show me how to create a profile. He made corrections on his quotes about his father. He was protective of his father's image. I had focused on his relationship with his parents and had hoped to show the reader how this created his tormented character.

Before each interview, Norman would excuse himself to go to the bathroom, magazine in hand. He was that tense and anal retentive.

In January Norman turned the PEN Congress into a celebration. Eight consecutive Sunday evenings in a theater on Broadway, famous writers read from their work. Before and after each reading there were parties at Gracie Mansion, at the U.N., at publishers' homes, at embassies. Friends of Norman's, the Steinbergs, gave a fundraiser. At the buffet table I ran into Sonia Braga and Robin Williams, my old friend from acting class. He was surprised to see me at the literary gathering and happy that I was now a writer. At Jean Stein's party after the Vidal/Mailer debate, attendees included Paul Newman and a bespectacled Warren Beatty. Warren failed in his attempt to look literary, but appeared to be succeeding in his flirtation with a female PEN executive—though he remained close to an exit. Warren signaled to me an awkward "don't tell me you're a writer!" hello as Norman peered out of the corners of his eyes while rattling ice cubes in his scotch.

One morning at a panel discussion, Norman showed up sporting two black eyes. "I was sparring with my son Michael," Norman said.

I didn't believe him. Neither did Page Six of the *NY Post*, which recorded his black eyes. Norman used Michael, his son with Beverly Bentley, as his cover whenever he got into scrapes. Michael was a good cover for him.

"If you need to reach me," Norman would say, "call Michael. He'll find me."

Forever stirring up controversy, Norman responded to a petition signed by writers that protested the appearance of Secretary of State George Shultz at the PEN Congress. "I didn't invite Secretary Shultz here in order to be insulted, to be, uh, *pussywhipped*," said Norman, whose quote made *Savvy* magazine, which chose Norman as "One of the winners, losers, and louses of 1986." (Not long before this dubious achievement, Norman had been selected as one of America's 10 Sexiest Men Over 60.)

Pussywhipped was a word I had taught Norman, who had wanted to know its derivation. I explained that when I met Rod Stewart, Rod was living with a domineering Britt Ekland.

"You're pussywhipped," I would tell Rod.

"Pussywhipped?" he would say, smiling.

When Rod ended his relationship with Britt, she sued him. Rod and I continued to date. One day he wrote the lyrics of "Hot Legs." During its recording session, Rod ad-libbed, "Are you pussywhipped?"

In 1985, Norman asked me, "Pussywhipped. What's that?"

"A wuss. Letting others push you around," I said.

Soon Norman was saying pussywhipped this and pussywhipped that.

Norman and I taught each other words. One of his favorites was "oxymoron." Soon I began saying oxymoron this and oxymoron that. And, indeed, Norman was an oxymoron—an overweight senior citizen who was one of the best lovers I had ever had.

Elle liked my profile and gave me another assignment to interview Chevy Chase, who was an old friend. Chevy was nervous for the interview and downed a beer to get going, but then it went well. We hadn't seen each other for a few years. When he married a girlfriend of mine, I was invited to the wedding and went to parties in their home in the Hollywood Hills. In the mid-seventies Chevy and I met backstage at *Saturday Night Live*.

Norman was proud that I had another assignment from *Elle*, but he was even prouder when my novel *Flash* was bought by Pocket Books. My agent was excited that they offered a sizable advance for a first-time novelist, but little did I know that when negotiating, my agent withheld from my editor the blurbs written by Norman and Gloria Steinem. I suspect my agent knew about Norman and me and felt that his blurb was gratuitous. Perhaps my agent felt that he did not mean his words and only wrote his blurb because we were having sex. I'll never know Norman's true feelings, but I do know I wasn't having sex with Gloria Steinem. Her blurb had been sincere. When *Flash* was published, my publisher put both of these blurbs on the front cover of the hardcover, but for the paperback put only Steinem's on the cover and Mailer's on the back.

Norman was especially happy about the advance money as I could pay my rent with it along with the few assignments I was getting. If I were tight one month for rent, he would help me out, but basically I was supporting myself.

I had to do rewrites for *Flash* while Norman prepared to direct *Tough Guys Don't Dance*. He would be coming to L.A. to do casting in the spring. I was thrilled that we would be together again and that our careers were moving along in unison. His love for me was proving itself in the success I was achieving as a writer and in his desire to be close to me as much as possible, though a nation separated us.

When my profile on Norman was published in *Elle* in January, I placed an item with a columnist to give it a mention. Norman and I garnered publicity. We were a team. That team I had dreamed of. That feeling of being on the same team that I had had with my father.

Pleased with the timing of these events, Norman called and said, "I'm going to do you a favor. Ever heard of *Parade*?"

"Vaguely," I said.

"It's a supplement in the Sunday *Daily News*. Has a huge circulation. Goes across America as it's syndicated. Its editor is Walter Anderson. I'm going to send you to him. I think he might like you."

"In what sense?" I asked, suspicious. Norman was frequently trying to fix me up with Mickey Knox, which infuriated me. I was not going to allow him to pass me around the literary world. But Mickey Knox was hardly literary. He was more concerned with the criminal world while feigning a career as an actor.

"Anderson's gung ho about this sobriety business and may want to give you an assignment," he said.

Sure enough, Norman made an appointment for me to meet Walter Anderson at the magazine the following week.

Wearing a red dress, red lipstick, and trying to dress as much like a journalist as possible, I arrived at the *Parade* office. A handsome and dapper Walter Anderson stood, extended his hand, and introduced himself.

"Have a seat, Carole. Norman told me you did a good interview with him."

"Thank you. It was my first," I said, hiding my trembling hand.

"What was the thrust of your interview?"

"Sobriety. I wanted Norman to talk about his drinking and the relationship it had to his parents."

"Are you sober?"

"Six years. My last drink was December 25, 1980."

"Congratulations."

"In 1971 I was on the covers of *Newsweek*, *Cosmopolitan*, and *New York Magazine* and felt like a failure. Today, not sure of next month's rent, I feel terrific."

"That's it. That's your lead sentence. I want you to write a story for us about your recovery from alcoholism."

I couldn't believe it! Norman would be so proud of me. Why, I was proud of myself. Norman hadn't told me what to say. He had gotten me the interview. Yes. But I had said those words.

When I told Norman about the assignment, he said, "See, I knew Walter would like ya, kiddo. Now get crackin'." Within three weeks I had completed the assignment, which Norman helped me to edit between his presidential duties for PEN.

A few weeks after I turned in my story, Walter Anderson called. "Your piece is good. I'm going to make it our cover story for June '87. I will be sending our photographer, Eddie Adams, to photograph you in L.A. I have your numbers and will stay in touch."

When I told Norman, he said, "How'd you pull that off?" He sounded a trifle jealous.

"He liked the piece," I said with defiance.

"He liked you," Norman said. "Pity it won't help promote *Flash*."

"How's that?" I asked, confused.

"You have two different readerships. The *Parade* article is sacrosanct, while *Flash* is pithy and sophisticated. Polar opposites."

I wasn't going to worry about it. I would be back on another cover. Oh, it would take a year to be published, but this was God's will.

I had hoped Norman would have been a bit happier about it. I had hoped his ego wasn't damaged by my success. His reaction made me wonder if he was hesitant about my succeeding on my own. It was one triumph to interview him, but another to interview myself and to be put on the cover of a magazine going across America with a readership in the millions. As it turned out, I received over ninety fan letters. Norman wouldn't read one.

In March of 1986 I returned to L.A. It felt good to be in my own apartment with my art collection.

Eager to continue with my fledgling career as a journalist, I called up an editor I knew at *L.A. Magazine*, told him about my *Elle* and *Parade* pieces, and began to pitch interviews.

Jerry Leiber and Mike Stoller were friends from my married days. Jerry and I met through Cy Coleman, the composer who had been my husband's best man. Jerry and Mike were preparing a show for Broadway called *Stand By Me*. This was news. My editor friend at *L.A. Magazine* agreed and assigned me to do a profile on them.

"Great you're writing, Carole," Jerry said to me. "That acting can fall off a cliff anytime. I hope you keep this writing gig up. You know so many celebrities. You could make a nice career out of journalism."

"Thanks, Jerry," I said. "But I'm only beginning."

"Become the new Barbara Walters! You can do it. You did a good interview and I've given many of them." Jerry Leiber wrote most of Elvis's songs, most notably "Hound Dog."

When Norman arrived in June, he helped me to polish the Leiber/Stoller piece. My editor was pleased with the results. Then I pitched an interview with Norman. The hook was his upcoming directorial foray. Norman and I did the interview in the Imperial Gardens restaurant at the foot of the Chateau Marmont. Again I allowed him to edit his quotes. He liked this. In fact he demanded this, but Leiber and Stoller and Chevy Chase never asked to edit their quotes.

L.A. Magazine was pleased with my work. I now had three clients. *Elle*, *Parade,* and *L.A. Magazine*. When Norman's interview was published, again I placed an item in the *Herald Examiner* mentioning our names. Our teamwork continued. Our merry-go-round in the press and in life.

Norman was staying at the Chateau Marmont. Here he chose to do preliminary casting.

In a phone call after our interview Norman asked, "Do you know any actresses that I might audition? There are two good women's roles, and since you were an actress, I'd like your input."

"I'm still a good actress."

"Look, I don't want to get into that with you." Norman said, lowering his voice. "I told you if you want to audition for a part, I'll put you on tape. Then I'll decide if I want you to read for the producer, Tom Luddy."

"Why do I have to audition? I have a reel of my acting work."

"All my actresses are auditioning. Norris did, and you must too. So what other actresses do you think I should read?"

"You could try Alana Stewart. Valerie Perrine. Candy Clark." Was Norman going to hit on my friends? I suspected as much, but never found out. Was I being used by Norman once more? He was doing so much for me by granting me interviews that I overlooked his Bluebeard side.

"I'll call their agents in the morning. Here's the script. Study it, and I'll put you on tape when you are ready."

I was not pleased with this charade. My sober friends thought Norman was giving me the runaround, but as usual, I trusted him and ignored his manipulation.

When I showed up at the Chateau for the audition, Norman was full of himself. He pranced around like Cecil B. DeMille without a circus. I went through the shenanigans once more, hating myself for it. This was a reenactment of his casting couch fantasy.

After this fake audition, which Norman conducted with utmost sincerity and without sexual innuendo, I made a feeble attempt to make love to him, though I was fuming inside because I felt he had put me on. I left in the middle of the night filled with self-hatred. How could I have allowed Norman to touch me after putting me through this charade? This was a phase he was passing through, I told myself. An old man living out a fantasy. If I wanted him in my life, I would have to understand that he was at a crisis. Being a director had been his lifelong dream, and he had to act out all the fantasies connected with this dream.

In my haste to leave, little did I know Michael, Norman's son, was in town and would discover that I had left my shoes in the closet.

Norman called the following morning. "Did you leave those shoes on purpose? Now Michael knows and could tell Norris."

"Of course I didn't do that on purpose. You just bummed me out with this audition crap."

"Well, if it's any consolation, your audition was good. I want you to read for my producer Tom Luddy, Fred Roos, who is casting the film, and John Bailey, my cinematographer."

"When will this big day be?" I asked, angry that I had to go through this nonsense again. Well, I didn't have to. I was going to. Simple as that. Norman had to feel he was the boss even if he wasn't. I was sure this was one of the reasons he stayed married to Norris. She gave him the impression that he controlled her life. Maybe this was why she auditioned too.

"If you're going to have a bad attitude, I won't audition you."

"I will audition," I said, "but I need to bring my own actor."

"Whom would you want?"

"Seymour Cassel is a friend. He's a good actor, and we can work on the scene together. This way I won't embarrass you."

"The actor who did all those Cassavetes films? Do you think he would do it?"

"As a favor to me. Yes."

"All right. In two days meet us at the studio. I'll call you back with the exact time and address."

I called Seymour. "Carole, I'll help you out. You know I will, but don't you see he's putting you on?"

"Whatever. I feel I have to do it."

"He's just getting his rocks off on your time."

"Seymour, he's an old man who's looking for his youth in this directorial fantasy. I love him and part of loving Mailer is satisfying his fantasies."

"Well, I'll be over in an hour, and we can run through the scene. But I'm doing this for you, not for Mailer."

When good-looking, virile Seymour Cassel and I showed up on the set, Norman turned crimson. He introduced us to Fred Roos, Tom Luddy, and John Bailey. Immediately we went into the scene. I was wearing a pink knit dress and no bra. Those were the days. And the "look."

The scene called for Seymour to kiss me. When he went in for the embrace, Norman began to rage. "YOU CALL THAT ACTING? BOTH OF YOU GET OUT OF HERE! I WANT REAL ACTORS!"

By now Tom Luddy, Fred Roos, and John Bailey had run out of the room.

Seymour and I fled. Norman's wrath was Technicolor.

Later I thought, though I hadn't gotten the part, I had gotten revenge. Seymour's good looks and virility had made Norman jealous when Seymour kissed me. Norman had wanted me to be his property. Had he told Tom Luddy, Fred Roos, and John Bailey about our sexual relationship? Had he bragged about how he controlled me? Had he bragged about how I had become his sex slave and that I wanted no other man?

When Norman called, he said, "Some trick you pulled. Embarrassing me in front of my crew."

"I didn't embarrass you. You embarrassed yourself."

"Why did you have to be different? Every other actress auditioned with the actor we hired, but you had to bring in your own lackey."

"I did you a favor. I wanted you to look professional."

"My ass. Well, you lost the part."

"There was never a part. You want Isabella Rossellini because you saw her pussy in *Blue Velvet*."

"I want her because she is a good actress, and you're not."

"She's got an Italian accent. The part is for an American!"

"We'll work around it."

"You don't care about me. You just care about pussy!"

"Horseshit!"

"Have you found the actress for the other part?"

"Not yet, but one of those Bond actresses came in and said, 'Who's dick do I have to suck to get this part?'"

"So did you give her the part?"

"I'm considering her. Oddly enough, she gave a good reading. We're not done casting."

Bet you're enjoying every lascivious moment, I thought, but did not say. I had said enough.

Later when I asked Norman if the Bond actress had gotten the part, he said, "No, when she auditioned with Ryan O'Neal, she wouldn't stop kissing him. I don't need that on my set." Miss Bond had fractured Mr. Mailer's ego and, therefore, had lost the part.

That spring, a backer of Norman's upcoming film gave him a party off Mulholland Drive to promote it. Norman had asked me to help him invite people. I suggested Swifty Lazar. "No," Norman said without explanation. I always wondered what rift there was between Swifty and Mailer. After my humiliation in the casting session, I made a feeble attempt to placate Norman and tried to invite a few celebrities I knew. Most weren't interested. I understood why he kept asking for my help with actresses for his film and for people to invite to his party. He did not have Hollywood clout. I was useful to him because I lived there. In 1986 I knew, to a modest degree, the inside machinations and social scene.

Shirley MacLaine did show up. She had a crush on Norman. One night a few months earlier, Norman had invited Shirley to Nicola's Restaurant in Manhattan. I don't think she expected me to be there, and throughout dinner she made it clear that she would have enjoyed going home with Norman. After dinner Norman said, "I'm glad that's over. She makes me uncomfortable. Oh, she's a pleasant lady, but not my type."

In the summer of 1986, after Norman left Hollywood, I began finishing my novel, *Flash*. It was due at the publisher in the fall. Norman did not have the time to give me any more editorial guidance because he would be in Provincetown. I was glad as this would force me to make decisions on my own. Also I began lining up writing assignments to cover the filming of *Tough Guys*. *Us* and *You Magazine* in London wanted me to do pieces for them. *New Woman* offered to fly me to Provincetown to interview Isabella Rossellini. I would query these publications by writing the managing editors and making a pitch while including clips of my work.

Norman's help with an interview with Isabella assuaged to a degree the rejection, humiliation, and pain I had felt during the bogus casting session. I knew I had been given these assignments because Norman had granted me access to his set.

Now, Norman and I were helping each other again and were back into that teamwork. My three assignments also were helping Norman garner publicity for *Tough Guys*. When the pieces were published, I contacted columnists and arranged press for Norman and me. I was beginning to feel like Norman's publicist. I didn't mind. In fact, I was proud to be associated with him, though Richard Johnson of Page Six had a problem with mentioning Mailer. For some reason, Johnson felt Norman was too self-serving in his press items. Happily, I was able to patch that up with Johnson, who wrote me a letter stating that Mailer had been reinstated in Page Six.

When I visited the set in Provincetown, Norman was in good spirits. He was accomplishing his fantasy. However, when I observed the filming of a scene between Rossellini and Ryan O'Neal, I noticed Norman was more concerned with their opinion of his direction than his opinion of their acting.

One day I went to see the filming of his lovely leading lady, Debra Sandlund, in a bedroom scene with Ryan O'Neal. Norman had "Closed Set" on the door, but I managed to sneak in. I wondered if there had been film in the camera, or if he was doing to Sandlund what Peckinpah had done to me with Jimmy Caan in *The Killer Elite*.

"What are you doing here?" Norman asked when he saw me standing in a corner. He proceeded to throw me off the set. We had it out in his trailer.

"What are you doing to that poor girl?" I asked.

"Directing her in a scene. As it's written."

"You're just getting your rocks off."

"If you continue to interfere with my directing, I'll have to ask you to leave Provincetown."

I left the trailer feeling horrible and ashamed and wondered why I had to invade Norman's space. Jealousy, no doubt. I had been wrong to question him, and that night at dinner, I apologized.

Shortly after this incident I flew out of Provincetown and back to L.A.

The following spring Norman took his star, Debra Sandlund, to Cannes for the film festival, which infuriated me. I was envious and wanted to be with him.

After Cannes, he flew to San Francisco for his film's post-production. I flew up from L.A., and we had another scene of our own.

"She was the star of my film," Norman said. "Get that through that thick head of yours. Norris wasn't even there."

"Oh, Norman, I just wanted to be with you."

"Your pressure is going to destroy us."

"I'm sorry," I said.

Once again I realized I had been wrong. It was easier for me to be jealous of Sandlund, who was a new beauty on his arm, than Norris for whom Norman's sexual attraction had faded.

The previous winter of 1986 Norman had wanted me to sign a paper stating that he would be paying my rent that year. Without reading it, I signed it. Beginning in January he gave me half of my rent. Then he stopped sending me the checks.

When I saw him that spring in San Francisco, I asked him about this.

"You got your money from your assignments. You don't need my money. When do you get the money for *Flash*?"

"I won't get it until fall when I turn it in. And what about that insurance policy you promised to get in the event of your death?"

"I've got to talk to Scott Meredith about that."

"You keep saying that, Norman."

"Well, I can't give you rent money now. I have the IRS to pay. Huge debt. And I can't work on my novel *Harlot's Ghost* because I'm busy with post-production on this film."

"I don't know what was written on that paper you asked me to sign, but I won't be your tax deduction unless you pay what you promised. I'll report you to the IRS."

Norman punched me in the stomach. I felt diminished. Less than. Bad. Did I deserve this physical abuse?

Why was Norman violent? Why did I put up with this? I couldn't leave him now. I had quit acting. My income was in his hands. Under his control. He told me he would help me become a writer so that he could create my dependency on him. My dependency on him allowed him to treat me any way he felt like treating me and get away with it. This abuse included using me for his many nefarious purposes.

Still I loved him. Why? I rationalized about his violence and told myself he couldn't help his anger and had poor impulse control—little control over his emotions. That *he* must have been abused himself. Somehow. I didn't know how, but it must have had something to do with his childhood. Was he still angry about all those enemas his mother had forced on him, which were violations of his body? His being? And did this cause him to be violent toward women?

I grew afraid of him, but still would try to stand up to him. Eventually I would fold and give into his will when his violence became uncontrollable.

From this date on we had fights over money and that paper I signed. I had never been given a copy of it. I realized why Norris was looking the other way while Norman and I were together. She and Norman needed me as their tax deduction.

My few days in San Francisco in the spring of 1987 were not pleasant. Our lovemaking suffered. Norris was flying in the day after I left.

Norman was a busy philanderer. He had stopped in Chicago to see the married woman he had had an affair with for many years. I rather liked that he kept such a long love affair active. It was romantic, and though we had begun having our quarrels, his lengthy affair with the woman in Chicago helped me to believe that he'd never abandon me. This thought assuaged any jealousy I might have had. I accepted Norman as a philanderer. I viewed true love as acceptance. I believed a person could love more than one person at a time. True love has few boundaries.

When I returned to L.A., I turned in *Flash* and the journalism I had gathered in Provincetown. Then I continued to work on a new novel I was writing, which Norman had begun to edit in San Francisco. It was called *Passwoman*, but it would have many titles. *Corporate Sex* and *She Looks at the Coffin and Smiles* were other considerations. It was about a group of powerful men who tried to pass a former schoolteacher among themselves and tried to impoverish her in the process. The protagonist, a rich and successful businessman, was at first English, then Hungarian. The novel was written in the first person, then third person, then half third person and half first person. Genet's *The Balcony* had been my inspiration, as well as Norman's treatment of me.

After *Flash* was published, I showed this novel to my editor, who said, "But *Flash* was so funny. Your second book I wanted funny. This is grim."

Finally by 1991, I realized Norman, with his contradictory editorial suggestions, had been jerking my chain. Eventually I finished this novel on my own. Today a copy of it is in my closet. The original manuscript is with Harvard.

Harvard (and my closet) also have a book called *How to Pick up a Movie Star Handbook,* which Norman began editing when we first met in 1984. It listed all the stars with whom I'd had sex. Norman suggested I give each star a number and call each one a case history. It was meant to be satire. Norman and I laughed a lot as he edited it, but the probability of getting it published was slim. He did send it to his sister who was an editor at Simon & Schuster, but they passed for legal reasons. Norman even edited this handbook over the phone from New York when I was in L.A., allowed me to tape his conversations, and chose photos of me to go with each chapter. I'll never know if he was putting me on.

In the end it didn't matter because with each lesson I was learning the craft of writing. I was grateful for Norman's lessons. He was giving his time and energy. It was the process of writing and his teaching that I sought, not the result.

Upon my return to L.A. from San Francisco in late May, I needed to see a gynecologist who said I had been given a venereal disease. "Your partner gave you trichomonas. He must take these pills."

"He's in New York," I said. "And married. I'm not having sex with anyone else."

"Well, his wife will have to get this medicine for him. He is a carrier."

When Norman called later that week, I said, "Norman, you have to see a doctor. You gave me something."

"It must have been the woman in Chicago," Norman said. "All right. I'll take care of it. Sorry about that."

Now I was more convinced than ever that he and Norris were not having sex because she would have gotten it too. When we had our tiffs, the thought crossed my mind to threaten to call Norris and tell her, "Your husband has a dirty dick," but I never did.

"When is the *Tough Guys* premiere?" I asked Norman.

"We're firming up the date. Late June or early July."

"I'm coming in."

"I wish you wouldn't. It's not going to be a big affair."

"Norman, I want to be with you for the opening. I want to see you. I feel a part of the film. After all the press I did—Liz Smith, Army Archerd in *Variety*, the *Herald Examiner*, Suzy in the *Post*. They're all writing up the pieces I did on your film."

"Have it your way. Where will you be staying?"

"With my friend, Betty Ann. On East 57th."

"I'll call you next week, angel."

Early in June of 1987, I was mailed an advance copy of my *Parade* article. There I was on the cover, smiling. I was pleased with how I looked after so many years. It had been a long time since I had been on a cover, and there was my quote, "I was on the covers of *Cosmopolitan*, *Newsweek*, and *New York Magazine*, yet I felt like a failure. Sixteen years later, not sure of the next month's rent, I feel terrific." The editor Walter Anderson signed it, "Carole, whose real image brightens the world. Yes, you can."

What an accomplishment! I wanted to show Norman, but couldn't call him.

When he saw my cover, he called me. "Well, chickadee, you look terrific. Now I'm glad you're coming to New York."

"See you soon," I said and blew him a kiss. "This is all because of you."

"You did it," Norman said. "This is your triumph'. Bye, angel."

Columnist Liz Smith wrote me asking to get together sometime in July and that she was happy to see that I was "on my way."

While preparing for my trip to New York, I invited my next door neighbor in to see my apartment and to keep an eye out for my possessions. I had an extensive art collection that she admired, leather designer furniture, Mies van der Rohe chairs, and Knoll shelves and table. My apartment building, called the Lotus, had been owned by Valentino and had a Shangri-La feel to its pagoda architecture. It was very old.

After I had been in New York for one week and had attended the premiere of Norman's film, which was uneventful as he had predicted, I got a call from my neighbor. "The Lotus burned last night. Your possessions are in danger. Mostly water damage, but you probably should come back to sort through what is there."

I began to tremble. I was uninsured. What was I to do? I cried. I prayed. I had invested all of my modeling money in my designer furniture and my art.

When I told Norman about it, he said, "Walk away. That stuff wasn't worth anything anyway." These words from the man who knew nothing about art. From the man who had to ask, which tie to wear with which shirt. Sure he would later write a book on Picasso, which he would ask me to help him research, but he had an enormous amount of help.

I looked at my *Parade* cover and thought. I did that. I can get over this fire.

Quickly I found a one-bedroom apartment in New York on West 56th Street near Carnegie Hall. I would come home.

Home to New York, where in 1965 I had come after leaving my family in Springfield, Pennsylvania, to become a stewardess for Pan Am, which allowed me to see the wonderful world and its many treasures. Home to New York, where in March of 1971 as a model I had been on the covers of *Newsweek*, *Cosmopolitan,* and *New York Magazine,* all in the same month. Home to New York, where in 1975 I returned after Claude Picasso jilted me in Paris. Home to New York, where the toilet paper was soft, not brown and scratchy as it had been in Paris. Home to New York, where in 1975 I had filmed *Stepford Wives*. "Don't go to Hollywood," my agent had said, but I had moved to Hollywood to test for a movie after leaving Claude. Now in 1987 my mantra was "Enough of Hollywood and its bad vibes."

Using my advance from my publisher, I furnished my new apartment. Norman offered no help there either. Once I had the basics, I flew back to Hollywood to put my damaged possessions in storage, where they would stay for six years.

Appraisers estimated my possessions to be worth half a million dollars. Norman had said my property was worth nothing. (I was beginning to think that is what he thought I was worth.)

I would have to continue with my new life in New York and try to think about the good things. Like my novel that was going to be published in the summer of 1988. For the rest of 1987 I would concentrate on journalism, study writing at Columbia and N.Y.U., and work on my second novel that Norman enjoyed editing, though I was getting a bit weary of his feigned help. Its plot was going in circles, much like Norman's when he had been drinking and writing. Still, I told myself his lessons were worth his manipulation.

I told myself to focus on journalism. Ahmet Ertegun, the chairman of Atlantic Records, whom I had met when I was engaged to Claude Picasso, was a friend. He introduced me to Julian Lennon, whom I interviewed for *Avenue* magazine.

Dudley Moore also was a friend whom I had met in group therapy in Hollywood. He granted me an interview for an English client, *Plus* magazine. A journalist friend had suggested I write to this publication and pitch articles. And so it went.

Norman was pleased that I was making money as a journalist. Getting him to help with my rent was a continual struggle. The fire had not made him generous. In fact he had become cheap, downright stingy, and would not allow me to order string beans as a side dish at a Chinese restaurant. My anger was festering when I realized how well Norman and Norris were living with their huge home in Provincetown, townhouse in Brooklyn Heights, and vintage Mercedes while I was being thrown crumbs and having to haggle him for half of my much-needed rent. But I was never a material person, I told myself. After all, I had left Claude Picasso *after* he had become a multimillionaire. I left him because he wouldn't set a wedding date. No, there were more important things to me than possessions. Learning how to write was one of these things that I cherished.

Still, I continued to enhance Norman's career with my interviews and by getting him press. He continued to help me by granting interviews. On a good day, when I wasn't trying to pay bills, I thought we were helping each other.

On November 4th, because of my *Parade* cover story, I was invited to speak at the eighth annual Conference for M.A.D.D., Mothers Against Drunk Driving, at Penn State, my alma mater. My mother, who was eighty-seven, came with me, and we had a wonderful time. I was able to put the loss from the fire into proper perspective. Material possessions. I had my mother, my good health, and much to be grateful for. It felt good to make my mother proud of me.

She didn't like Norman and used to say, "I don't know what you see in that old geezer. I really don't."

During the winter, I studied at N.Y.U. with Margaret Atwood, whom I had met at the PEN Congress, and Gordon Lish at Columbia. Lish read my chapter on my father and said, "You should be writing nonfiction, with the experiences you've had!"

Shortly afterwards, while crossing the street on the way to lunch, Norman put his arm around my waist.

"You never did that before in public," I said.

"I love your spirit, and I just want to tell you how pretty your pussy is. It's prettier than all the pussies I've known." Then he paused and said, "You should write fiction like me. It's too hard to write nonfiction."

Flattering my pussy to keep me from writing about him. That's a new one. Sex with Norman had lost its initial passion, but we still made each other feel complete. With the publication of *Flash* on the horizon, Norman was prouder of me than ever. These feelings added to our sex life, which had been damaged by the fire and by Norman's abuse of me during the casting of *Tough Guys*.

One day I did say, "Norman, I have to tell you that I don't get turned on by those scenes you like to act out. You know, like the 'casting couch.'"

"Look, darlin', we don't have to do that if you don't like it."

Another day, I came out of the bathroom, and Norman had one leg in one of my stockings and was about to slip on one of my high heels. "Norman, that's not my thing," I said to a forlorn Norman.

"Fine," he said. "Just thought we could have some variety." He was good-natured about my rejection of his fantasies, though I wondered if deep down I had damaged his self-image as a "macho man."

In June of 1988, *Flash* was published and to a great deal of press and hullabaloo. *The Philadelphia Inquirer*, *People* magazine, who ran four pages, and *Newsday*, who put me on the cover of its magazine section, all did profiles on me. In 1993, because of my profile in the *Washington Post*, Oprah Winfrey's show called to have me as a guest about former models, but I had to decline as I was dealing with the fire in L.A. at the time. As it was, in 1988 I did seventeen talk shows largely because of the success of my appearance on *Larry King Live*. Larry King predicted on air that I would be doing many talk shows.

"Get your publisher to do a satellite interview," Norman said, though I noticed an air of jealousy in his voice. "That's what Random House did with me." His suggestion was ridiculous. I was not a big enough author to warrant this.

"I'm not you, Norman," I said.

The *Publishers Weekly* review was good, while *Kirkus* wrote, "*Flash* has a buoyant, likable heroine who grows—not just in spite of her sins, but because of them."

"I guess they liked what I wrote about your novel, kiddo," Norman said, pleased that *Kirkus* had agreed with him.

USA Today wrote, "Mallory describes sex and the emotional desperation it breeds perfectly. The result is pruriently hilarious."

The Daily News wrote, "Mallory turns the screws on Hollywood in this deft, sophisticated read."

MS in London wrote, "Her short, sharp one-liners ricochet raunchily off the page."

When my publisher gave me a book party at Elaine's, Norman said Norris had to go to Arkansas to be with her parents. It was again apparent that he was controlling her, and she was on the leash that he held. A dog's life, Mrs. Norman Mailer's was. We were in the same kennel.

I was pleased that celebrities came out for my cocktail party. It felt good to see novelist Jay McInerney, filmmaker and photographer Gordon Parks, media mogul Mort Zuckerman, Warhol collector Jane Holzer, former supermodel Marisa Berenson, journalist Joan Juliet Buck, child psychologist Dr. Lee Salk, composer Cy Coleman, Nancy Reagan confidant Jerry Zipkin, and Norman's son Michael Mailer.

My close friends came too and that made me happy and proud. My best friend, Heather MacRae, who was the daughter of Sheila and Gordon MacRae, agreed to a photo with Jay McInerney, Norman, and me that made *People* and the *New York Post*. Then there was Betty Ann Grund, the editor with *Elle* who kindly gave me my first assignment as a journalist. Graciously, Betty Ann had offered her apartment on Sutton Place for matinees with Norman. The Elaine's bash ended at about 9:00 p.m., and Edie Baskin, who was the ice cream heiress, gave me a dinner party downtown.

Norman didn't come downtown after the cocktail party at Elaine's. I always assumed he went off with someone he met at the party. I didn't berate him about this, nor was I sure of it. It was simply something that I suspected. I was getting too much attention for his fragile ego and was unable to focus on him. This could have driven him to seek attention elsewhere.

The next morning Norman called. "Well, that was some party last night. You had quite a turnout."

"Why didn't you come downtown with my girlfriends?"

"I had to take Michael home," Norman said, though I remained convinced this was not the truth.

"When are you taking my editor and me to lunch?"

"Next week, or do you go to L.A. then?"

"No, I go in two weeks. When do I see you?"

"Oh, I'm deep into my novel, but I suppose I could squeeze you in tomorrow, kid," Norman said, then laughed.

When I saw Norman, I felt that we made love. He was proud of me and treating me with respect, which nurtured my good feelings for him.

Not long after this, I flew back to my former home, Hollywood. My good friend Berry Berenson gave me a dinner, hosted by her husband Tony Perkins. Superagent Sue Mengers came, as well as Paul Jasmin, who had played the voice of Tony Perkins's mother in *Psycho*. Berry and Tony were great friends of mine. A few years later, he would die of AIDS. Then she would die in one of the doomed planes that flew into the World Trade Center towers on 9/11. A tragic end to the parents of Elvis and Osgood Perkins, their handsome children.

I went from dinner at Berry and Tony's to dinner at Patrick Terrail's, the former owner of Ma Maison restaurant. Patrick wanted me to meet Gigi Gaston (Getty), whose father was Jean Paul Getty Sr., and Margaux Hemingway. Patrick had been a friend of Claude Picasso's mother, Francoise Gilot.

All this hobnobbing with old friends was fun and stimulating, but there was nothing that beat sitting down at a computer, pounding out a story line, and having my weekly conversations and matinees with Norman. I became homesick.

In July of 1988 I happened to look at the *Star* while at the supermarket and noticed my name linked with Michael Jackson's. London's *News of the World* had published that I had been in an orgy with Tatum O'Neal, Leif Garrett, and Michael Jackson, whom I had never met. I called Page Six to disclaim the article and said that someone in London was capitalizing on the recent British release of *Flash* by writing lies about Jackson and me. Then I sued the *Star*, but never saw any money from it—one more instance of lies printed about poor Michael Jackson.

Once back in New York for the duration of 1988, I threw myself into my journalism. I did a piece for *Vogue* about putting collagen in my lips, which I titled, "A New Lip on Life" and a piece for *GQ* called "Quit Line to Me" about lines men handed women. Norman didn't want me to do the *GQ* piece because its editor, Art Cooper, had put me on the cover when I modeled. Norman felt the stigma of having been a model had affected his vision of my skills as a journalist. *Vogue* never published the piece because I had mentioned it to the press prior to publication. I hadn't understood the sensitivity of magazines about publicity.

Then a new magazine called *Buzz* gave me an assignment to interview David Puttnam, who had been the head of Columbia Pictures in the mid-eighties. Warren Beatty was instrumental in getting David fired from Columbia when David complained about the losses of *Ishtar* due to Beatty's spending. When I was engaged to Claude Picasso, I met David. In the late eighties he was living in England producing films to follow his success with *Chariots of Fire*. "Keep up the writing," David said after he read *Flash* and gave it a blurb. Today, he is a member of the House of Lords.

In 1989 I read that an old friend, Oscar-winning director Milos Forman, had a film about to be released. His version of *Les Liaisons Dangereuses* was about to hit the screen, and he wanted publicity. "It's good to see you succeeding in writing, Carole," Milos said. "That acting is tough when you don't live in Hollywood. You have good instincts as a journalist." I interviewed Milos Forman for *Smart Magazine*, whom I pitched by querying the managing editor. With all of my clips, I was able to get assignments without Norman's clout. Even without his interviews. This felt good; though I remained grateful to Norman, who had created the journalist in me.

Norman and Milos were friends, and I had the feeling Norman would have liked for me to have a fling with Milos, but I was too focused on Norman. One night after having had dinner with Milos, as we were walking along 57th Street, Milos met Mikhail Baryshnikov. Milos invited Misha back to his apartment, which was not far away.

We all sat in comfortable leather furniture. Milos loved comfort. He made us drinks as I asked Misha, "What are you up to?"

"I'm preparing *Metamorphosis* for Broadway. Kafka."

"I want to see it."

"Come as my guest. Of course."

When I left Milos's apartment, I had the thought to interview Baryshnikov. The next day Norman called. "Great idea. You could do a good interview with Baryshnikov," Norman said. "Write your editor at *Parade*. Who is it, David Currier? Try to get an assignment."

In April of 1989 *Parade* assigned me to do a profile on Baryshnikov. Now I had to get him to agree to do it. "He's wiry and elusive," Norman said, shouting. "Don't fuck this up by bringing your girlfriends backstage. Go alone for Christ's sake!"

Misha had gotten me two tickets for his performance on Broadway, and despite Norman's warning, I invited my girlfriend, Debbie. Norman didn't want to go, but said he'd go at another time.

After Misha's brilliant performance, I took Debbie backstage. I was intensely attracted to Baryshnikov and felt I needed Debbie as protection against my sexual urges and flirtations. I couldn't tell this to Norman. I wanted an interview with Misha. Period.

"Welcome, Carole," said Misha, who wore only a baby-blue terry cloth robe. I introduced him to Debbie.

"You were incredible," I said.

"How did you two meet?" Debbie asked.

"We met through Mike Nichols at that art opening," Misha said. "How did you meet Mike, Carole?"

"I dated him in the mid-seventies. He took me to Jackie Onassis's anniversary party at El Morocco. We were photographed by *Life* magazine."

"Brag, brag, brag, Carole," Misha said, smiling as I couldn't help noticing his bare feet. They were beautiful. Perfectly formed like an exquisite line drawing by Picasso.

"Debbie used to date Milos," I said as Misha's eyes grew wide.

"Ah, you two compare notes!"

Debbie asked Misha to sign her program. He threw it on the floor.

I ignored his tantrum. "I can cut the interview in two ways," I said, trying to get him to agree to be interviewed.

"Listen to the hustler," Misha said, then showed me a perfume bottle. His perfume. "Nice, pretty, no? It's George Barrie. Fabergé. That's who left."

"When does it come out?"

"June."

"I was the Tigress girl in the mid-seventies."

"Really?" he said, matter of fact.

"I did a striptease for the Tigress TV commercial." I realized I was talking too much about myself. "Are you in pain?"

"A little," he said. "My back."

"Were you making those sounds?" I asked.

"Yes." Misha made a cricket sound. "All right. I do interview. GO!"

"Sorry, Misha, Debbie and I must leave now," I said, laughing.

He laughed too.

Debbie looked on, bewildered.

The next day I called Misha.

"Thanks for last night," I said.

"My pleasure," he said.

"I was preparing your interview."

"When shall we do it?"

"I'm not going to psychoanalyze you. Just talk into the tape."

"Same old shit."

"Don't worry, Misha. Norman Mailer says I'm a good interviewer. He says I listen when I'm paid to listen."

"Then we should hang up."

Norman called the following morning. "So how did it go with Baryshnikov?"

"He'll grant me the interview. We went by his dressing room after his performance, but I didn't take my tape recorder."

"You're crazy! You always take your tape recorder! You let someone hold it in the background if necessary."

"I took Debbie..."

"Well, you're an asshole. You have an interview to do. Stop taking care of your friends. You're giving Debbie a big pleasure. It's ridiculous. If celebrities sense you are unprofessional, they feel uneasy, and they don't want to give you an interview."

"He said he'd call today and that he wants to do it tomorrow. He was tired. I didn't have my questions prepared."

"I'm going to be tough on you professionally because there's no excuse for it. You should have been prepared!"

"Don't worry. He'll call. You think I could have blown it?"

"When you're getting an interview with someone who's difficult and tricky, you have to have your tape recorder because you never know when lightning strikes. Come on, seize the opportunity. You're an opportunist. Don't be a fucked up opportunist! Okay, I'm tired of yelling at you."

"Say you're sorry."

Norman laughed. "I don't want to say I'm sorry. That would be a lie. I'll try not to repeat it in a hurry. All right?"

"I hope I didn't blow it with Misha."

"You can do such a good interview with him. Just relax and get your questions in order. How was *Metamorphosis*?"

"It's long. No break. But he's very good."

"I'm sure he is. His movements are beautiful."

"He moves like a rooster and makes sounds like a bug. A cricket."

"Maybe I will see it. He's such a talented man. All right. Okay, babes."

"Thanks for the coaching. I love you."

"See you soon, dear. Bye, bye."

Misha called the next morning at 11:30. "What you do?" he asked.

"I'm waiting to interview you."

"Can you be at ABT downtown by noon?" he asked.

"How's one o'clock?"

"See you then."

When I arrived at the studio, Misha ordered tea and behaved as though it were an honor to be interviewed. He didn't make faces or growl or pretend to be rude as he had backstage. Misha answered all of my questions and was most touching when he talked about his mother. He was the perfect gentleman and talked to me for two hours.

A few months later when a *Vanity Fair* journalist flew to Japan to interview him, Misha walked out of the interview moments after it began.

To my surprise and disgust, *Parade* didn't put Misha on the cover. He was given two pages in the back of the magazine while I had been given four pages and the cover. This didn't seem right. I asked Norman about it. "We're seeking good relations with Russia," Norman said. "It was political."

But in September of 1989 Liz Smith wrote as a headline in her gossip column, "Carole, a hot writer getting hotter. Carole's novel, *Flash*—a kind of female Terry Southern workup—has become a cult hit. Now for *Parade* we see Carole on the high wire with Mikhail Baryshnikov. He discusses his father, 'A rough man, but you don't teach your parents how to live.' His mother, who committed suicide: 'I'm not accusing anybody of my mother's death. She never had a chance. There was nowhere for her to go.' His own courage, 'Aw, come on. I don't have much courage. I just do what I want to do. What excites me. I've had a great life on stage, but I think this is not accomplishment. To go through life is already one big courageous thing.'"

When David Currier, my editor at *Parade*, approved my piece on Misha, Norman sat on the bed and listened on the other phone. He was so happy. Like a proud parent. I had my answering machine on and had accidentally taped Currier's words. "Keep that recording," Norman said. Currier said that I had done a good interview.

Norman cared about my work, but with my growing sense of independence, which was a result of the success of my journalism, I was feeling less passionate about him.

Chapter 17

On June 7, 1989, to my surprise, Baryshnikov invited me to the ballet. He gave me great seats. After the ballet, I met him on the stage. "Now don't start dancing," he said, smiling as he went off to talk to the dancers, and I went home alone.

Later that week the paperback of my novel was published. Norman had chosen Gallaghers for lunch. He let out a sound when he first saw me. "Oh.... You look like Jackie Kennedy." My dress popped open from laughing.

I handed him the paperback of *Flash*.

As he looked at it, he made another sound, "Oooooooooooh."

"Is that you on the cover?" he asked.

"Yes," I said.

"Where's my quote." He studied my photo.

"On the back."

Norman wanted it on the front.

"Don't do TV to promote it," he said.

"Why?"

"I could never have married you. You ask too many questions."

"Is that why I'm a good interviewer?"

"Don't do TV because your book is literary. Good writing. Your publisher never marketed it right. And don't talk to the press about your affairs with stars. That will discredit you."

"You told me to say I was addicted to having sex so they wouldn't try to say I was a flasher."

"Well, I've changed my mind. But don't do TV for the paperback."

Listening to Norman's advice, I foolishly refused to do television talk shows to promote *Flash*. This alienated my publisher.

After lunch, Norman went to his studio to write while I went to Saks to do a photo shoot with Baryshnikov. He was there promoting his perfume. He put his arm around me and pushed aside the woman from Fabergé who tried to block the photo. "Aw, come on," he said. He did two photos with me. Then he squeezed my waist. And I never saw him again.

I wondered if I had done the right thing to take Debbie backstage as my bodyguard. While I will always have a warm place in my heart for Misha, I know I had made the right decision to ignore his flirtations, difficult as this was.

My experiences with Norman were teaching me that sex and business do not relate, but I had to learn the hard way. In 1989 I pitched an interview with Norman to *Smart Magazine*. Until this exchange, interviews had been a game to us.

"Don't show me your questions," Norman would say, running to the bathroom before I would turn on the tape recorder.

Norman was early for interviews and often arrived before the designated hour of our weekly matinees. "Sorry I'm early," he would say. Sometimes he brought me flowers.

By surprising me, Norman was encouraging me to do the same. During our *Elle* interview in 1985 he told me, "I like women who surprise me. When we have something serious with a lover, it's important to keep it alive. Only bullies, tyrants, fascists like the predictable."

While Norman could be the bully and the tyrant, he did not like the predicable. By seeing me only once a week, he kept our attraction alive. He was a well-traveled philanderer who confessed to having had seven serious mistresses.

During our first years together, I felt Norman loved me. Oh, I know he liked looking at my body and hurried to see me because he wanted to see what I was wearing, which had the promise of a guaranteed erection. This meant everything to Norman. His ego and self-worth were in his erection. He enjoyed prancing around with it and displaying it like a proud stallion looking for a mare. No, Norman never had a problem getting an erection. Not with me, but I admit that those outfits, besides showing a desire to please, were my form of control. My attempt to tame a literary wildman. Yet there were days when Norman didn't want to have sex and only wanted to talk.

While Norman was educating me, I was hoping to instill in him respect for a woman to whom he was sexually attracted. One of my questions in interviews was, "Does a man's sexual attraction for a woman threaten his respect for that woman?"

"Not if it's real," Norman would say, laughing. "Don't ask me to explain real."

Each day Norman read the gossip columns and was thrilled to see his name in print. He called me when his name was mentioned.

"Don't you think the writer and the novel are two separate products?" I asked Norman in our 1989 *Smart Magazine* interview.

"Ideally, the media should have nothing to do with literature, but it does. It's gotten into the critical synapses."

"You're not telling me that Tom Wolfe's white suit doesn't help him to sell books?"

"No! No! Tom Wolfe happens to be a very good writer. The white suit has something to do with how bad he is when he is bad. There is something silly about a man who wears a white suit all of the time, especially in New York."

Tom Wolfe answered Norman's accusations on Page Six. "The lead dog is the one the other dogs always try to bite in the ass," Wolfe told the *New York Post*'s Richard Johnson.

Norman called me from a pay phone to read me this item, then rushed over to our apartment. I don't think I'd seen him happier. "I've got to write a rebuttal," he said wide-eyed, rubbing his hands together. "Get me a pen."

"Don't forget to give me credit for the interview, Norman."

"You're not a part of this anymore, dearie. This is between Wolfe and me."

While I understood Norman's point, I didn't understand his enthusiasm. I had queried *Smart Magazine*, conducted the interview, called columnist Richard Johnson at the *New York Post*'s Page Six, and now Norman was elated to eliminate me.

Norman's behavior was emblematic of how he treated me during our relationship. Once my purpose had been served, I would be eliminated. In 1989 I was oblivious to this. I dismissed Norman's behavior as self-centeredness.

Page Six printed Norman's retort: "I would remind Tom Wolfe of the companion to his old Southern saying. 'While it is true that other dogs will always try to bite the lead hound in the butt, it doesn't mean you're top dog just because your ass is bleeding.'"

Norman was thrilled that his photo appeared above this item and also thrilled to have had another opportunity to attack Wolfe.

Press meant a great deal to Norman, and he did a great deal to get into columns. But he was smart enough not to let anyone know how much he cared about the media and the degree to which he orchestrated what was written about him.

Norman was a challenge to interview. When he became irritable, it was because he had difficulty translating his feelings into words or because he feared his image might be in jeopardy. When Norman spoke, I could see by his expression that he was visualizing his words as they would be written. I tried to jolt him out of this calculated rigidity through provocation and humor.

Only when I was able to shock Norman or make him laugh would he stop watching his dialogue as though it were on a stock market ticker tape. Our interviews appeared to be a form of torture until I was able to make Norman laugh. Spontaneity only happened when Norman was provoked into forgetting himself.

In 1990, as he was finishing *Harlot's Ghost*, Norman had a writer's block.

"Are you thinking too much before you write?" I asked. "Don't watch yourself. Just put it down, then edit."

"Are you teaching me how to write?" He laughed, then admitted that he had been doing just that.

Our interviews were good when they took the form of sparring and repartee as in the *M Magazine* piece and half of the *Smart* interview.

For those subjects, when provocation was inappropriate, gentleness helped Norman to reveal himself. He seemed to want to expose his past pain through me if I led him delicately. Sometimes I felt as though I were a conduit through which Norman's bottled-up feelings were conveyed. Or that during interviews I had become his pencil.

My presence never had the permanency of pen.

Norman taught me to shape each interview and to ask the tough questions at the end of the interview because the subject could walk. I placed my questions about alcohol at the conclusion of my interview with Norman. In later interviews I would ask those questions when I felt Norman had said something funny and was feeling good about himself.

After our interviews, Norman liked to futz around with his grammar, but the quotes that he changed were about Barney Mailer and Abbie Hoffman. In my original transcript for our *Smart* interview, Norman had said that he believed Abbie had been murdered. Because he felt he could not substantiate his belief, he changed his statement to, "I think it was suicide, but if they waited three days to decide that Abbie had taken 150 pills, it was because the case was so big and the local coroner was scared."

I allowed Norman to edit his text on this interview and the *LA Magazine* interview. He knew he could get away with altering his comments because he was sleeping with his interviewer, but after 1988 I stopped letting him get away with that.

Having a publicist would not be good for Norman's literary image. Marketing savvy was not part of being an artist.

"You ought to consider doing PR," Norman would say to me.

I only liked doing publicity for him and for my other interviews. There were days when I questioned whether Norman preferred the love we shared or the publicity I generated for him.

Not all magazines held esteem for Norman. I tried to protect him from those rejections. After Norman stabbed Adele, he believed he had been ostracized, but that was untrue. It was Adele who had been ostracized. It was as though he were *untouchable*.

Because he was obsessed with public opinion and his image, in 1989 in my *Smart* interview, I asked Norman, "If you feel this hateful toward the media, why does it love you so?"

"I have nothing to do with it," he said. "I could spit in the mythological eye of the media every morning. They would still love me."

Yet why was Norman so anxious to edit his quotes? Kurt Vonnegut and Joseph Heller had not asked to edit their quotes. Nor had Baryshnikov, Dudley Moore, Isabella Rossellini or Milos Forman.

No, Norman had a great sense of his place in the media and had a great deal to do with it. Also he knew changing quotes in an interview was unethical, but that he could get away with it with me. I was new to journalism and did not know protocol. When I understood that Norman was taking advantage of me, I stopped allowing him to edit his quotes.

Consistent with his calculated image, Norman's opinions were often based on the political correctness of the time.

During our *Smart* interview in 1989, Norman said, "Warhol, who possibly had less to say as a painter than almost anyone around, is treated as a great painter. It's absurd."

But in an interview in 1994 Norman said, "By now, Warhol is seen as a great artist even by people who do not profit from such an evaluation. He is the maggot genius of American culture."

Only Graydon Carter, the editor-in-chief of *Vanity Fair*, exposed Norman. Literally. In the early nineties when Carter was the editor-in-chief of *Spy* magazine, he published a photo of an overweight Norman Mailer mooning toward the camera. Trick photography. When I asked Norman about this, he laughed and never mentioned it again.

Norman knew to ignore something he could not control and that giving attention to negativity gave it power.

Norman was more upset with Philip Burke's cartoon of him in July 1991's *Rolling Stone* than his bare-buttock *Spy* photo. He was furious with editor-in-chief Jann Wenner for an innocuous drawing of him with his hand on his knee while wearing a short sleeved t-shirt and a quizzical expression. His nose was broad as it was. His eyes were squinting. His ears jutted out perpendicularly. I couldn't see what disturbed Norman. Sometimes I thought when Norman Mailer looked into the mirror, he saw Paul Newman. Forever wise with his marketing, Norman never complained to Wenner. Instead, in the presence of this powerful and affluent editor-in-chief, Norman was complimentary.

Norman's behavior was similar around Terry McDonell, who then was the editor-in-chief of *Esquire*. In 1991 when Norman met McDonell at a cocktail party, shortly after McDonell had published *Esquire's* cartoon of Norman kissing Gore Vidal (which had infuriated Norman), he was gracious.

While Norman's anger toward these influential editors raged in my presence, he would curry favor with them in their presence.

By the end of 1989 I had found a new client, Jane Lane, the editor of *M* magazine, a Fairchild publication. Jane was a good editor and became a good client who assigned me interviews with Gore Vidal, Kurt Vonnegut, and George Plimpton.

First she assigned me an interview with Norman, which she called "The Power of Sex." Though she had put him on the cover, she did not give me a byline.

"Your editor made it look like I've written for her magazine," Norman said with contempt. After he read the interview, he said, "This is one of the best interviews I've given. Norris said, 'The Power of Sex is you, and I have the checkbook.'"

He laughed. I didn't.

This was the first time I had not allowed Norman to edit his quotes. He was angry that I had turned in the piece without allowing him to see it, but when it was published, he agreed that I had done the right thing.

Jane Lane had asked for half the amount of words I had submitted, but she published the entire transcript for a whopping $10,000. It was a great piece—if I can be excused for saying so myself. So good that Norman's army had raised their weapons and were about to wage a war against me. He had lost control over me. Finally I was growing up. His lessons were manifesting their result in my becoming the journalist he had wanted me to become.

When Norman first read my interviews, he liked them. A few days later, he would relay the feedback of his children, his wife, his agents, his lawyers, his publisher, his publisher's publicist. The extended family realized they were in my target zone. Though Norman liked our interviews in published form, he was not a man of his convictions. The keepers of his flame had decided that he was revealing too much to me.

Norman Mailer was a cowardly literary lion.

Part of being a good journalist was being informed. I read the papers daily, and one day I noticed Gore Vidal was in town to promote his latest novel *Hollywood*. Quickly I called my editor to find out if she wanted me to interview him. She loved the idea. Now I had to get Gore. The paper had said he was staying at the Plaza Hotel and was about to fly to L.A. In my haste I wrote a note to Howard Austen, who was Gore's longtime companion.

Howard and I had met in Hollywood in the late seventies when I had dated Peter Sellers. Howard had a keen sense of humor, but was protective of Gore. I knew Norman's interview with *M* would be on the newsstand in the hotel lobby and that they probably had seen it.

After I dropped my note at the Plaza, I called Howard.

"Thought you were an actress," Howard said.

"No more. Did you see my interview with Mailer?"

"Yes. Gore is reading it now. He'll grant you the interview, but we're flying to L.A. tomorrow."

"Let me get back to you. *M* may pay my airfare."

My editor was thrilled and said she would fly me to Hollywood where she would put me up in the Beverly Hills Hotel.

"How'd you pull that off?" Norman asked before I left.

"I knew Howard Austen from my acting days and had met Gore in Hollywood years ago. I always had a crush on him."

"Bizarre. Anyway good luck. He's very difficult."

"So are you."

"When will I see you?"

"I'll be back in four days. Wish me luck."

"Get your questions organized. Don't be slipshod with this. But I know you can do it. Ciao, dear."

At the Polo Lounge, Gore showed up on time and was a gentleman. "We met here in the mid-seventies with Lester Persky and Truman Capote," I said to him as I studied his full lips and listened to the sensuous timbre of his voice. "Lester was taking me to the Oscars for producing *Shampoo*, but he was drunk. Truman said to Lester, 'You're too drunk to go to the Oscars and...'"

"I wasn't talking to Truman then," Gore said, cutting me off, but no one attacked more than Norman. Norman's growling had taught me not to react to Gore. Norman had helped me to develop that thick skin, which I needed for Gore. For all my interviews.

Gore was nice once I allowed him to attack me and did not try to defend myself. I had let him get his angst out. He could see that I would permit him to dominate the interview.

During the interview, Gore mentioned Norman's name as if Norman were in the same room. I assumed Gore knew about Norman and me. Afterwards, Gore even agreed to be photographed with me. It was a good day and a good interview.

When I returned to New York, I placed an item with Page Six. On March 26, 1990, the *Post* reported that *M Magazine* had flown me to Beverly Hills to interview Gore Vidal, who was promoting his latest novel, *Hollywood*. The *Post* wrote:"'Can you believe it?' gushed the curvy Carole. 'Eliza Doolittle interviewing Moses.'"

Norman called as soon as I returned and wanted to know how it went.

"Good, Norman, but he kept talking about you as if you were there. He must know about us."

"It's a small world, Carole. I keep telling you that you and me, kid, are a hot item. We have to keep a low profile because if the papers ever got wind of us, there would be no let up."

It felt good to hear Norman's voice and to be held by him. But I was beginning to feel like an old married wife. I watched him with my third eye as we made love and wasn't really there. He didn't know his cuddles were the best part, that afterwards I felt so loved. Serene. I didn't understand those good feelings, though. I didn't have an orgasm. Maybe I was changing. Hormones, that is. Or relaxing. Sex seemed to be in my head. I knew where Norman's was.

We lay in bed, listening to the stereo. "Next I think you should interview Kurt Vonnegut," Norman said.

"I don't know him."

"Give me the phone."

Norman called Kurt Vonnegut, who said, "I hear Carole's interview of you was good." When Norman hung up, he said, "Call your editor and get an assignment to do Kurt. I think he'll grant you an interview. He asked that you call him tomorrow."

The next day my editor gave me the assignment, and I called Kurt, who said, "Your interview was good, but then Norman's a good interview."

"So are you," I said.

"When do you want to do the interview?" Kurt said. "Wednesday?"

"When do you go away?" I asked.

"Thursday."

"Do you have to pack?"

"You aren't planning to camp out are you?"

I had a week to read as many Vonnegut books as possible and get my questions organized. Kurt lived next to Katharine Hepburn on the East Side of Manhattan. He also had a home in Bridgehampton, which later I would visit. Books lined the interior of his townhouse. Its condition was a bit chaotic, but not sloppy. His wife was photographer Jill Krementz, and her photos were everywhere.

Kurt gave me two hours, and like Misha, answered all of my questions. Saying he was funny is an understatement. So is saying he was nice. Prior to his writing career, Kurt had worked in PR and knew the value of publicity. He was a shark when it came to promotion. While he was going through a divorce with Jill Krementz, which never materialized, Kurt and I became friends. Norman would have liked to have seen Kurt and me as a romantic couple, but this never happened. I'll never know if this was to titillate Norman or because he cared about my well-being and knew Kurt would take care of me when Norman ended our affair. This would absolve Norman of any guilt for what he intended to do with me after using me for nine years.

When I turned in my piece, my editor liked it. It was so long that I was able to cut a second one from it for a West Coast publication called *Exposure*.

Norman read the final interview and said, "You really read Kurt. Now how do you feel about doing George Plimpton?"

"I know George," I said. "I'll have to see if my editor wants him."

Within a few weeks I had done the interview. Norman liked it.

"I feel I didn't read George Plimpton," I said.

"He's not that good a writer," Norman said.

In the summer of 1990 I had the idea to interview Joseph Kennedy II in conversation with Norman for *Men's Life*. This would be the first of a series of dual interviews I would conduct. Because of Gore's interest in Norman when I interviewed him, I also pitched to the magazine an interview between Gore and Norman. Norman liked both ideas. Then Norman suggested I ask his son Michael to talk to Joe Kennedy II. Michael knew Joe from Harvard. Joe consented to the interview. This was beneficial not only to me, but also to Norman, who had never met Joe. The Kennedys' approval meant a great deal to Norman.

Meanwhile my editor, Barry Golson, had given me a few questions to ask about Joe's father, Robert F. Kennedy. Fearful of upsetting his social relationship with the Kennedys, Norman asked me not to ask any "hard questions."

At the end of the interview, feeling that I had to do my job and honor my commitment to my editor, which Norman had taught me to do, I asked Joe about his father. Joe walked out of the room in a huff with Norman running after him. Later, Norman lambasted me for my doing what I thought was right and for doing what I had to do as a journalist.

The interview was sadly never published, as *Men's Life* went bankrupt just before publication. I had used a lawyer to draw up a contract and managed to be paid $15,000. I wanted to give part of my salary to Michael for his help.

"Don't you dare," Norman said. "If Michael ever needs money, he knows he just has to ask."

After this interview, I wrote to Gore in Positano, Italy, asking if he would do an interview with Norman. Months went by with no reply.

In late August of 1990 Norman had the idea that I should interview Bill Styron. I had several phone conversations with him. He was elusive, to say the least. I was trying to get him to grant me an interview for *Architectural Digest*. The magazine had said that they would give me the assignment if I could get Styron's permission to do his house in Connecticut. The magazine would also assign me to do Norman's home in Provincetown, along with an interview with him, if I could get Norman's permission.

When I asked Norman about this over the phone, he said, yelling, "Is that Paige Rense? She's been trying to get my house for years. Do Styron instead of me."

"Doesn't Styron have two houses?" I asked.

Norman dodged the question. "I thought you would like each other," Norman said. "Bill is sensitive like you. He has a nice voice, doesn't he?"

"Yes," I said and hung up. I knew Norman's game was to fix me up with Styron.

Styron, whom I had met several times, liked me to talk to him about alcoholism. Or so he led me to believe.

As it turned out, Styron, Mailer, and *Architectural Digest* had all been putting me on.

After the success of our *Smart* and *M Magazine* interviews, my feelings of being used by Norman were confirmed when Norman asked me to ghost his self-interview for *Cosmopolitan*. Norman had told me he could not understand Helen Gurley Brown's questions and needed my help to rephrase them. After we completed it, he said he was pleased with his phony self-interview for *Cosmopolitan*.

I wasn't pleased because he wouldn't give me a byline and because he was able to turn me into an employee by paying me $1,000.

Originally *Cosmopolitan* had wanted to excerpt second serial rights of my *M* interview, "The Power of Sex." I was told by a fellow journalist that foreign rights were worth between $2,500 and $4,500. For the piece alone I had been paid $10,000. But Norman's agent, or Norman, had convinced the magazine to commission him to do a self-interview about sex so that he would get this money and pay me a fraction of my worth while eliminating my byline. After the interview, Norman *again* asked me if he could claim me as a tax deduction.

When Norman and I made love, Norman frequently became childlike. So did I. Sex was experimentation. Games children would play. Doctor, nurse, vet, garage mechanic, plumber. Norman and I had fun playing follow the leader. Norman and I liked to laugh about sex.

One day a boyish Norman said, "My anus is my vagina. You have yours, and I have mine." He would pose naked on all fours. Norman's literature is filled with anal references, especially *Ancient Evenings*.

When our affair was new, Norman would come to me in need of a bath. "Norman, I won't make love to you unless you wash," I would say.

"But that's natural body odor," Norman would say. He would rub his hand under his armpit, place it under his nose, inhale, then sniff. "Hum, what a pleasurable aroma."

"Norman, it's not your armpits that offend me."

"Body odor should be celebrated. You read *Ancient Evenings*. Honey Bee's lust for human fragrance."

"Bathe or I'm not making love to you."

"You have no sense of culture," he would say, defeated. "I'll take a bath if you give it to me."

So every few weeks, a grungy Norman would arrive, and I would have to talk him into allowing me to bathe him. He needed this ritual.

One day I asked Norman, "Why do you pretend not to want me to bathe you?"

"My mother would bathe me. I guess that's part of it."

"All mothers bathe their sons."

Norman's ambivalent feelings toward women appeared in our first interview for *Elle* in 1985. I had wanted to explore Norman's feelings toward his parents. Norman held back about the abusive nature of Fanny and Barney's relationship and Barney Mailer's alcoholism. "My mother was terribly practical and hardworking," Norman said. "She had circles of loyalty. The first loyalty was her children. The second was her sister, her family. The third loyalty was her husband."

Norman felt that his mother loved him more than her husband. Was this reality or Norman's Oedipal need? Norman was attracted to strong women who reminded him of his mother. Eventually their strength repulsed him and recalled his mother's smothering love. Gradually Norman would try to destroy these women. As our sexual attraction waned, and I gained more independence, I felt Norman was trying to destroy me. I became more afraid of him.

In our *Elle* interview I asked if Norman's propensity for parties got in the way of his writing. "No question it does," he said.

About this time, Norman wanted me to interview Gay Talese, whom I knew. In fact, Gay had been hitting on me for years since my married days in the early seventies. I had hoped Gay had outgrown his juvenile need to seduce every woman he met, so I agreed to do an interview. He came to my apartment, and the interview went well. When we finished, Gay said, "Well, shall we go to your bedroom?" I threw him out of my apartment and wondered what Norman had told Gay.

When Norman called, I shouted, "I'm sick of your trying to pimp for your friends, Styron, Talese, Mickey Knox. And using my desire to be a journalist as a hook for your childish need to pass a woman to feel macho. You ought to be ashamed."

"Look, dearie, I was just trying to help you get interviews with these men. I never said anything to imply that you were a good lay."

"Don't talk to me like that. I am not an object!"

"But you've been one all your life. Why change?"

I was livid and was realizing Norman would not change. My love for him had been one-sided. His love affair with me would last as long as I was useful to him. Yes, I had wanted something from Norman. Writing lessons. His wisdom. But turning me into feelings of being his hooker damaged my loving feelings for him.

Aware of the fragile bond between Norman and me, a gay friend of mine who was a biographer said, "Carole, I hope you're keeping a diary."

Of course I was.

Chapter 18

One afternoon in 1990, Sylvia Miles, Geraldine Smith, and I were lunching at a restaurant in Midtown Manhattan. Sylvia and Geraldine were actresses who knew Norman from the Actors Studio. Being around actors stimulated Norman. He would direct young actors in the Directors Unit. Both women knew about my affair with Norman.

During lunch Sylvia turned to me and said, "I hope Norman is wearing a condom."

I was offended. "Why do you say that?"

"With AIDS, my dear, you must be careful."

I knew Sylvia was trying to warn me. There had been rumors that Norman went to the Actors Studio to pick up men.

Not long after this luncheon, Norman made his weekly visit to our apartment. During sex I said, "Norman, I need to ask you to wear this." I handed him a condom.

"You know I detest those things."

"We need to be safe. AIDS is all around us."

"How would you or I get AIDS?"

"I don't know, but I don't want to take any chances. Please put this on."

Norman slipped it on and lost his erection. "Sorry, but I feel trapped in one of those things. Smothered."

"We can do other things," I said as I fondled him.

He looked lost and rejected. Norman and I kissed, cuddled, and remained intimate, but I stopped allowing him to penetrate me. I felt sorry for Norman. He was sexually frustrated each time I saw him. I felt more like his caregiver than his mistress. I wondered again whether he was having sex with Norris. I doubted it. We no longer had sex because Norman would not wear a condom. That was his choice.

Too late I would realize that, with certain select friends, Norman was slandering me behind my back. But while we were together he would impress upon me that I should be indebted to him because he allowed me the privilege of interviewing him. When one of my professors, Gordon Lish, who was an editor at Knopf, gave a lesson at Columbia University during which he criticized Norman's sentences, I was shocked.

Norman didn't like people who saw through him, like Gordon Lish and Don Hewitt, the producer of *60 Minutes*. Norman loathed the esteemed news program because it reported that Norman did two books on Marilyn Monroe for money.

Norman had taken my income from the *Cosmopolitan* interview. He had thrown me crumbs and then had the nerve to tell me he was doing me a favor. I had the feeling he wanted to see me destitute. Then I couldn't write about him and his tricks and games and endless manipulation. He didn't care that I had lost all my property in the fire. He knew I couldn't keep earning enormous amounts on freelance journalism. My financial well-being was at his fingertips.

Just as my income and my work were being converted to Mailer's, so was my identity. I had been giving my life to Norman and had been trying to rescue him from his alcoholism at the same time. Nine years of sitting by the phone each week while waiting for his calls. Not having sexual relations with anyone else. There was no one else that I had feelings for...except Misha. And I had chosen to interview him as opposed to having sex. My life was now focused on becoming a journalist, a writer. But Norman was defiling me to Styron, to Talese, to Mickey Knox, probably to Tina Brown and to Harold Evans too. He had been sabotaging my years of good work. Like a giant steamroller, the Mailer Machine was denigrating, defaming, and destroying me with its power. While all the strings around me were being pulled delicately, it was Norman Mailer who was my puppeteer.

While Norman was pocketing income that should have been mine, as he did with the *Cosmopolitan* piece, he would ask how much money I had in my bank account. How much money my mother had in her savings account. It was as though he was planning to abandon me and wanted to know if my mother had money to care for me because he wasn't going to, despite his promises to put me in his will.

He would claim he wanted to help me, but he was trying to control me. By keeping me dependent on him, he believed I would do what he wanted me to do. I had defied Norman by editing the *M* interview and by submitting it to the magazine without allowing him to change his quotes. It proved to be a successful piece of journalism without his edits. I had defied Norman by asking Joe Kennedy II the questions my editor needed asked. A year later, in 1991, again I defied Norman after the Vidal/Mailer interview by not allowing him a second chance to edit his quotes. Vidal edited his quotes only once. Norman become irate. Then Norman claimed that I favored Vidal in the Mailer/Vidal match. He even blamed me for *Esquire*'s cartoon of him kissing Gore. *Esquire* was "outing" Mailer, not me.

By 1990, I realized Norman's writing lessons were his way of controlling me. I had written the second half of *Flash* without his edits. Determined to edit my journalism alone, I would not allow Norman to touch my pieces on Baryshnikov, Gay Talese, Kurt Vonnegut, George Plimpton, Milos Forman, Gore Vidal, Warren Beatty, and Madonna. I wanted to be able to love Norman without being dependent on him. But he didn't want me to have my independence. This made me feel smothered. Cheated. Disrespected.

Not allowing Norman to correct my work made him feel powerless. He needed the attention that I gave him during those writing lessons. He was not getting that kind of respect from many close to him. The keepers of his flame. His writing was business to them. It was his ability to earn them money that was their concern. I learned the more people knew about Norman, the less they respected him. This saddened me. I didn't want to lose respect for Norman, though over the years, I did too. My love eroded, turned to anger, then to pity. Norman was propped up by those around him who meant more to him than me because they, indeed, were his identity. I began to feel as though I had been duped into thinking that Norman Mailer was the Great One. I felt betrayed. But it was my own doing. I had put Norman on a pedestal, and now it was crumbling around my pen.

Norman's mantra was André Gide's words, "Don't be so quick to understand me."

I followed this advice and took nine years to understand Norman Mailer. Because of my alcohol support group's encouragement of introspection, plus years of therapy which I now question, it was my habit to try to understand what made people tick—especially Norman.

My desire for freedom threatened Norman.

"I can't be alone," Norman would tell me.

Again I felt sorry for him. He was such a little boy wrapped up in all that braggadocio. In the beginning I had felt that I could nurture him into feeling good about himself, but my nurturing had been futile. I should have been nurturing myself.

The next day he would say, "Carole, I worry about you. Your life is so limited. You have nothing. No one."

I would look at him and think, "I have you." But did I? Was he trying to tell me that he wasn't there for me? And never would be?

Going to parties, lunches, and having a chaotic lifestyle were of little interest to me. I wanted serenity. Experiencing life with Norman Mailer made serenity and its freedom all the more desirable.

Norman's definition of love was being willing to die for it. Love to Norman was a merging of identities, not a respect for a partner's uniqueness. If these differences were eradicated, which Norman tried to do to mine in our relationship, the remaining soul would be a mirror image of Norman.

This would explain why all of Norman's marriages failed except the one to Norris Church, who said, "It's true in a sense that everything I am today is because of Norman."

While I agree with Midge Decter that Norman invented a character whom he married, I believe the character he invented was not a woman, but Norman Mailer. According to *The Guinness Book of Names*, Norris is a boy's name.

The person Norman loved had to mirror Norman's identity. This guaranteed that the person Norman loved would never be able to abandon him.

"You will always be trying to dominate yourself; the woman you love will only be an instrument for you to practice on." Henry Miller's words from *Sexus* were quoted by Mailer in his *Genius and Lust*.

I recalled the time Norman had wanted to make love to me in the "inversion machine." I had been his instrument to practice on. I had allowed it. Had Norman been dominating himself?

I know Norman wanted his cronies to believe that I was his sex slave. "Volunteer," I would say, smiling. Until I suspected Norman's scam to impoverish me after he asked about the amount of money my mother had and his refusal to help me after the fire and to win a fair settlement that I needed for my twilight years.

In *Genius and Lust* Norman wrote: "Henry Miller screams his barbaric yawp of utter adoration for the power and the glory and the grandeur of the female of the universe, and it is his genius to show us that this power is ready to survive any context or any abuse."

Abusing the women he loved was Norman's way of relating to them and gave him pleasure. Compassion gave Norman power to abuse further.

"The worst things happen to you, and you bounce right back," Norman would say, smiling.

He loved testing my resilience. I would pride myself in what I thought to be stoicism while unknowingly I had deprived Norman of the pleasure of my suffering.

In September of 1990, when he had converted my fee for the *Cosmopolitan* interview into his money, I was unable to see that he was trying to destroy any financial independence I had so that I would not leave him—until he was finished with me.

With each interview I learned more about Norman's demons. His ghosts. The more I was potentially dangerous to him. The more danger there was that I would have the power of becoming his mother. And of writing a true portrait of him.

Further destruction to my identity became apparent when I realized the "spin" put on our affair by the keepers of his flame. It was that I was using Norman for his power.

I came to realize that I was in a relationship with a man whose desire to destroy was camouflaged by his charm, his wit, the power of his fame, and his obsessive love.

Norman's tragedy was that there was no other way for him to be. He lacked the courage to seek psychiatric help or to join a support group of recovering alcoholics, even though the doctors had told him he needed to do that after he stabbed Adele. Psychiatrists had said Norman was an alcoholic who needed AA meetings.

My tragedy was that I was codependent on him.

Ironically, while the gossip was that Norman Mailer had done my work, by ghosting his self-interview for *Cosmopolitan,* I had done his.

I only wish I had realized the tragedy that Norman was plotting before it happened. I was too naïve and focused on rescuing him, while he was too much the multi-faced devil focused on destroying me.

Chapter 19

In December of 1990 my *Cosmopolitan* interview that I ghosted for Norman was published. That Christmas he gave me a VCR.

"He's going to ask you to rent porn films," said a friend who knew Norman.

"No, he won't," I said, insulted.

After the VCR was installed, Norman said, "I'm going to rent us a porn film because I've been getting such a good response from your *Cosmo* interview."

"Forget it," I said. My Christmas present from Norman had been *for* Norman.

One trip to a porn theater with Norman had been enough. During the movie, he sat mesmerized. His lower lip hung forward much of the time while beads of saliva gathered on its rosy, thin skin. Every so often he moved his mouth in a chewing gesture. Norman, the genius, had detached from Norman and his penis. Pink flesh excited him as though it were fast food. While an actress performed fellatio, Norman placed my hand inside his unzipped trousers. Without looking away from the screen, he said, "She reminds me of one of my wives."

I withdrew my hand and refused to return to a porn film with him.

During sex, Norman had made me feel wanted. Flattery, his weapon. In the porn film he ignored me. I felt alone, like an object. A hand. Though I would struggle not to be an object to Norman, he was unable to relate to me in any other way. His flattery confused me and temporarily made me believe he loved me. It was difficult for me to believe that Norman could be as satisfied with me sexually as he appeared to be and not care for me. Today I wonder if Norman was ever able to have a sexual relationship with a woman without viewing her as an object? It would be less painful for Norman to have sex without feeling. Less chance of hurt. Of abandon.

He felt he could support or ridicule my writing depending on the advantage he could gain from his opinion. Behind my back, I had been told Norman denigrated me as a writer to his friends. This made me angry.

Norman demanded loyalty from everyone around him, but the narcissist was rarely loyal. Some of his friendships may have appeared to be based on loyalty, but a scrutinizing eye could see the reasons for many of his loyalties were the uses Norman could make of them. "Everyone uses everyone," he would say.

Norman's mother had taught him that he had to make the most of every moment, every opportunity, if he wanted to be accepted and be loved.

Norman rarely talked about being a Jew, but when he did it was without pride.

Today I know that Norman's way of profiting from someone was to make it appear that he was doing that person a favor. Just as by giving me the VCR, he had made himself a gift of it in order to turn me even more into an object. Through my writing I had been trying to free myself from having been an object, which was the reason I loved to write.

Part of my attraction to Norman had been the respect he could give me by educating me so that I could write about my experiences from exploitation to self-awareness. But as Norman began to know me better, his exploitation got worse because he grew closer to me emotionally and thus had more power to hurt me. During our nine-year affair we had developed an emotional relationship besides our sexual one. I believed my Pygmalion had grown to respect the mind he had educated. By 1990, he had come to value and to seek my opinions and my help as he had with the *Cosmopolitan* interview.

When I made love to Norman, I felt he made love to me. I believed Norman's charm and flattery were demonstrations of caring. My lack of guile and my innocence allowed Norman to use me. As a farmer, my mother had been raised to respect the soil, hard work. She did not have time to read and did not have role models to give her respect for literature. Because she spoke another language, Pennsylvania Dutch, she was ridiculed. "We talk half-ass-backwards," she would say. “Outen the light” meant put out the light. “Dumbkoff” meant dumb head. My father used this word to belittle my mother. Soon my mother felt stupid, like a “dumbkoff.”

My father loved books. Words. His desk was his altar. After his lobotomy, his sentences made no sense. My mother had to take charge of the family. Now the power of words only reminded me of the injustice of my father’s inability to express himself.

Though I had graduated from college and had become a teacher, I did not have the intelligence to defend myself against the manipulation of Norman Mailer’s genius. He was pleased that I was just another fawn in his deer park. Just another “dumbkoff.”

“You’re not very good at manipulation,” Norman often said about me.

On January 26th Paul Newman had a birthday party that Norman attended. The next day he called. His voice was filled with excitement. “Last night I ran into Gore at Paul Newman’s birthday. He will do the interview tomorrow. Can you be ready?”

“Of course,” I said. I had been reading his work for several months and prepared my questions in the event that “lightning would strike,” as Norman called opportunity.

“He’s staying at the Plaza. Drop him a note as to where and when with your number. I’ll call you later in the day.”

Quickly, I called the Plaza and booked a suite, which they offered to give me for no charge as he was a guest. It was clear that they wanted to please Gore Vidal. Then I called a friend of mine, Bettina Cirone, who was a member of the paparazzi. She agreed to do the photos on spec and would arrive at 10 a.m.

Gore showed up on time. Norman was early. I was nervous, but had my two tape recorders ready to go. There were no fisticuffs. Both of them were gentlemen, though guarded. They seemed happy to see each other.

“All you have to do is turn on the tape recorder. There’s nothing for you to do with this interview,” Norman said with confidence as he insulted me.

By his remarks Norman demonstrated that he had no respect for me as a journalist, but I continued to ask my questions anyway. I had over thirty questions and had been reading as much of Gore’s work as possible to prepare for this moment.

Feeling beaten down, I went deep into myself and found the confidence to begin the interview. My questions focused on alcoholism. Why Gore and Norman drank and the damage to their lives due to drinking. Norman had stabbed Adele in a drunken rage. In his book *Conversations*, Truman Capote claimed Gore had been thrown out of the White House by Bobby Kennedy when a drunken Gore insulted Jackie Kennedy's mother.

I turned on the tape recorders and began with my questions. To both Gore and Norman I asked, "To what degree has alcohol wreaked damage in your lives?"

Gore Vidal said, "Mercy. What a question. Like Winston Churchill, 'I have taken more out of alcohol than alcohol ever took out of me.' That's a direct quote."

"I don't drink at all."

"Oh, you don't? Since when?" I asked.

"About a year and a half ago," Gore said. "I have perfect recall, though. As drunk as I have ever been, I have never blacked out. And I can play back the tape the next morning—everything I said and did. And before I get up, I have to redo the tapes, edit them so that I can get up. I never lose a line. I remember it all." (By tapes Gore meant his memory.)

Then I asked Norman, "Have you ever regretted your behavior as a result of having had too much to drink?"

"I don't regret it, because I think I would have been dead of cancer twenty years ago if I hadn't been drinking," Norman said.

After the interview, Norman felt I had favored Gore and ran off in a huff.

"What's wrong with him?" Gore asked.

Norman had inscribed one of Bettina's wonderful photos with the following jealous words:

> "Dear Carole,
> To that happy couple, Gore and Carole
> Cheers, Norman."

At all times Norman needed to be the center of attention, and if he wasn't, he would have a tantrum. Like a child.

In February 1991 the Vidal/Mailer interview was bought by *Esquire* at auction. Editor Terry McDonell asked me to write a few words as an introduction, describing the feud between Gore and Norman.

"Can you tell me about your feud, Norman?" I asked.

"Go to the library. Jot down a rough draft for your editor, and I'll fact check it."

I did as Norman asked me to do. When I showed it to him, he punched me in the stomach and raged. "You can't turn that into *Esquire*. Let them do their own fact checking."

This was the second time Norman had punched me in the stomach. There was the other time in San Francisco. And now. I was numb. What had I done to deserve that? I had done a great interview. Asked his input about what to write in the introduction. Yet he punched me because I hadn't written what he wanted me to write. He viewed me as an extension of him. I still had no identity. He had no respect for me. I had no respect for myself to take this abuse. Still, I felt I needed him. I felt helpless without him. Lost in a world filled with literary pretense. Lost, period. I had made him my world, and now that world had been shattered. Norman never apologized.

Beaten down again out of fear, I did not turn in a prologue. I never wrote for *Esquire* again, though the interview garnered a great deal of press, and I had been paid $20,000 for what Don Hewitt thought was a good piece. After I mailed Hewitt the interview, he sent me a note, "Nice job."

Romance between Norman and me was now fractured. With this incident, and my not allowing Norman to penetrate me because he wouldn't wear a condom, he was feeling that he was losing more control over me than ever. His macho self-image had been pierced. I couldn't risk getting AIDS from him and had stood up for myself. I resented his bullying, but could not stand up for myself against his wrath.

In the spring of 1991 a French publisher contacted Norman about writing a chapter in a book about museums.

"I want you to come with me to the Metropolitan and ask me questions about Picasso," Norman said. "They want me to write about the museum, but I want to focus on Picasso's work. Interview me, tape me, and take notes. I'll pay you. It'll be a job. I like the work you did on my *Cosmo* interview."

"Norman, you don't know anything about art."

"They want my opinion. What can I tell you?" Norman chuckled. "You taught art and knew the Picasso family. Your help would be appreciated."

"Okay, I'll help you," I said, wondering what scheme Norman had in mind now.

The idea of Norman writing about art amused me. I knew the publisher wanted Mailer's fifty-cent words and his name, but did they realize that he needed to ask Norris or me what shirt went with which tie?

Norman flew to Paris and had a chat with the publisher. When he returned, he called me immediately. "I'd like to see that chapter you wrote about Claude Picasso and 'the family'." Norman laughed. "And Pablo."

"Why?"

"That book on museums has turned into a book on Picasso."

Just as *60 Minutes* had reported, Norman knew how to turn a small interest in his work into a big profit. He knew that the fame of Picasso meant he'd get a bigger advance than if the book had been on a museum. Norman knew the value of his work in the marketplace as well as the value of those about whom he wrote.

"What about my involvement?"

"Darlin', there's no need for you. Sorry. I'll be doing the book in Paris."

"I can get on a plane."

"I don't need you. I told you."

"You don't need me, but you need my writings about Picasso. Thanks, Norman."

"Don't be like that."

"Like what? You plagiarized Maurice Zolotow's writing on Monroe, and now you're asking me to cooperate with you stealing my life?"

"I don't want Claude. Nobody cares about the son. I'm doing a book on Picasso."

"If nobody cares about Picasso's son, why do you want to read my writings about him?"

"Background."

"Ha! And where's my present from Paris?"

"I didn't get you a thing. You had me in such a foul mood over that Vidal interview. I don't want to talk about this anymore. By the way, I'll be reading from *Harlot's Ghost* at the Y on February 14th."

"I'll be there. Tape recorder on."

"Gotta go, sweet pea."

"I love you. Perfume or no perfume."

"I got you a bottle of Chanel Number 5 last trip."

"Monroe's favorite. Did you know that?"

"I do now. Now let me hang up."

"I think I love you anyway."

"Goodbye, angel."

In 1991, during Norman's reading at the 92nd Street Y, half the audience walked out. He read on. I recalled the second time I had met Norman. That snowy night in 1984 when he had lectured at the Thalia. Much of the audience had walked out.

Norman walked off the stage then returned. He hadn't changed. I had. I was beginning to understand why people lost interest in him. With dignity and in his well-modulated voice, Norman read, "It was a long urination."

I wondered what Gordon Lish would have thought of that sentence.

"Everyone has the right to be offended, and everyone has the right to be offensive," Norman said with joviality as his fans pushed toward the exit.

Revulsion seemed to be the trademark of the Mailer audience, yet they kept coming back to hear and to see Norman Mailer in the flesh. Hearing Norman's love of the outrageous, and the press he sought while feigning not to be a part of its orchestration, had made Norman not a prisoner of sex, but a prisoner of fame.

That June of 1991 *Vanity Fair* flew Norman to L.A. to do a profile on Warren Beatty. At the same time A.S.C.A.P. flew me there for a tribute to songwriters Leiber and Stoller, whom I had interviewed.

Vanity Fair put Norman in the Bel Air, his favorite hotel. A.S.C.A.P. put me in the Roosevelt Hotel in Hollywood. Norman had the better accommodations; I had the better pool. David Hockney had painted a mural on its bottom that made swimming in this pool better than going to a museum.

Norman never would swim at his gym in Brooklyn. "With all that piss from the kids," he would say. Nevertheless, he would don his snorkel and goggles and float for half an hour face down in the Bel Air pool. With no Hockney painting to gaze at, no fish to catch, why did he wear a snorkel and goggles? I'll never know. They did help him to shut out everyone and every sound.

Norman reminded me of a floating armadillo. The thick skin he had earned as a writer became apparent when he snorkeled. He was an island in the Bel Air pool and in my life. He had allowed me to visit him for eight years. He had finished this chapter. We were entering the final round. He knew the clock was ticking. The alarm about to ring. He didn't care. He snorkeled on. He had everything under control, as usual.

I didn't like watching him swim. I could see how materialistic the writer-of-the-people-for-the-people was. Had the man who had written *The Armies of the Night* and *Why Are We in Vietnam*? cared about the issues in these books or were these tragic events in our American history mere fodder for his pen—just as *60 Minutes* had implied. His armor was thick. His fat, insulated. His wealth, protected. His fame, defended. As I watched him swim, I could feel how insignificant I was to him. All that flattery and Barney Maileresque–charm during lovemaking disintegrated when Norman snorkeled. It was the real Norman Mailer. In all his gear. Self-sufficiency. Dead weight.

In that summer of 1991, during what would be (unbeknownst to me) our last rendezvous at the Bel Air Hotel, I was being given a glimpse of how bourgeois Norman Mailer really was. How cushioned his life was. How he ate Chateaubriand, not plain steak. Those holes in his sweaters were to disguise his love of the bourgeois and the complacency of his overprivileged life.

When Norman gave his undaunted support for "the greenmailers" (folks like the Steinbergs) who offered what they had the audacity to call "their money" back to PEN, but who really wanted to advance their social standing, the real Norman Mailer was exposed.

Kurt Vonnegut railed against the greenmailers in my *M Magazine* interview with him. "Our country is going to go bust. These guys (these greenmailers), take care of the company by giving it to themselves and their friends. They practically write their own paychecks. After they get rich, they want publicity, too. They want to become famous for their generosity. An awful lot of them bankroll PEN now."

After he read my interview with Vonnegut, Norman was furious with him. Vonnegut, a former public relations director for G.E., also knew how to manipulate his press, but Vonnegut was not a social climber. Vonnegut would not allow PEN, which represented a writer's freedom, to be bought by greedy greenmailers who had taken freedom from others.

However, Norman liked to go to the parties of these wealthy social climbers. He liked their friendship, which helped him to wield power in certain circles and to make a nice profit in the process.

As I watched Norman snorkel, I thought that he would have made a good French king. A snorkeling Napoleon. How he loved his own power. His image. His phone book. Rolodex. His island.

Things had changed from the idyllic moments we spent together in 1984, when we first made love and passion was imprinted on this hotel's bedsheets. Instead, I preferred swimming in my pool with David Hockney and the few leaves that had fallen from the palms.

As I watched his giant body swim, puff, paddle, ignore, I wondered who he really was. Had I been making love to someone I loved? Or had I been making Norman Mailer into someone I wanted to love?

We ate in that same dining room where years before I had protected an elderly, vain Norman who couldn't hear the maitre d'. Because he had wanted to impress me, he had not wanted to make an issue about his hearing loss.

In 1991 he no longer cared about my feelings for him. He was now smug and knew that I was under his control, though my journalism was successful. He knew he could pull the plug on his help for me at any moment and damage my career.

After all, he had said of himself, "I'm like an old police dog in publishing. No one comes near my block."

Still Norman Mailer cared about my opinions. He wanted to know what I thought of Warren Beatty. What I thought of all the stars I'd had affairs with. What I thought of his publisher's publicist when he did not send me a galley of *Harlot's Ghost*. What I thought of his son Stephen's performance in the film *Cry-Baby*. What I thought of Gore Vidal, William Styron, Kurt Vonnegut, George Plimpton, Joseph Heller, Gay Talese.

With all of Norman's seeking of my opinions over nine years, had I gained his respect and lost his love?

But now after spending the day interviewing Beatty, Norman was restless.

"How did it go?" I asked.

"He's so guarded. I don't know what I have. I'm having trouble."

"Make it funny, Norman, or you'll get killed."

"Norris told me the same thing."

"You can't write that Warren Beatty's nice. Make fun of yourself. Like you did in *The Armies of the Night*."

"That's what I'm going to do. Now you'll tell me it was your idea!" Norman pouted.

"I'm just trying to help you."

"You realize I could be having dinner with Jack Nicholson and Warren Beatty, but I'm having dinner with you!"

The next morning Norman called me at my hotel.

"Carole, I'm seeing Warren in half an hour and wanted to know if you had any ideas about how I should get him to open up?"

"Get him to talk about his mother. Father."

"What about them?"

"Warren loves his mother and hates his father, an alcoholic. That's why Warren doesn't drink. He has other addictions. You should understand them."

"Thanks. Come over this evening about seven."

"I don't know when the A.S.C.A.P. event is over. I'll be by after it."

"Okay."

"Good luck! Don't be afraid of Warren Beatty, Norman. And make sure he does the talking!"

Click.

Norman was in a state from June to August while writing the profile on Beatty.

In one phone call Norman asked, "Do you want me to mention your name in the list of women Beatty's been with? It's easy enough to do. Here's the list: Natalie Wood, Brigitte Bardot, Jane Fonda, Joan Collins, Michelle Phillips, Whitney Houston, Elizabeth Taylor, Diane Keaton, Carly Simon, Julie Christie, Diane Sawyer, Goldie Hawn, Catherine Deneuve, Faye Dunaway, Elle Macpherson, Diana Ross, Janice Dickinson, Melanie Griffith, Dayle Haddon, and Annette Bening. You'd be in good company."

"That's just the celebrity list. What about all the other women he's had?" I asked. "What's good about being exploited?"

"How could these women be exploited? They consented. They're famous."

"Fame doesn't insulate someone from heartache. They're women with feelings. Like you and me. Well, me anyway."

"Now you're getting me in a foul mood. I just called to ask if you wanted to be in my piece."

"Sure, why not?" I said. "That's a wonderful group of women. I only wish we could all sit down in one room and talk about our experiences with Warren and how we really feel about his treatment of us."

"I'd like to be in that room with a tape recorder," Norman said, laughing. We hung up moments later.

Then I reflected upon the image of Norman snorkeling. How insulated he was. That island of self involvement, narcissism. The bulbous mound of bourgeois flesh feigning to be a writer for and about the common man, when all he really cared about were material possessions and celebrity. Was I one more name on a list of women in his life? As inconsequential as that?

Chapter 20

When Norman returned from interviewing Warren Beatty in Los Angeles, he began preparing the publicity for *Harlot's Ghost*. One morning he called to find out if I had received a galley from Random House.

"Norman, it hasn't come."

"This time I'm furious! I'm really mad 'cause twice I've put your name in and twice nothing's happened. Bob Lucid is my biographer, and I had to ask the publicity department twice to send him a book."

"That's disrespectful. Insolent. You have better things to do with your time."

"Exactly. Do you realize we agree on something for once?"

"Harold Evans mentioned your novel to the *Times* today. It was a good item."

"Good item? He said *Harlot's Ghost* was funny!"

"Isn't it?"

"A thirteen-hundred-page novel about the CIA described as funny? Evans wants it to be funny! I've got to talk to marketing."

"Don't you like Harold Evans?"

"I like Joni Evans."

That June of 1991, before Norman went to the Cape for the summer, we had dinner at a restaurant called the Symphony House. Again Norris was conveniently "out of town."

As we walked into the Symphony House, we met Jackie Mason at the bar. His bodyguard stood nearby. Mason's skin was white—as though he needed a transfusion. While his jokes were funny, his need for a bodyguard wasn't. Why should a comedian need protection? Norman introduced me to him. In my usual inept attempt at humor and without forethought, I extended my hand. "I'm the second Mrs. Mailer," I said.

Norman's face became flushed. A glazed expression came over his eyes. He turned morose. When we were seated at our table, I said, "I'm sorry, Norman. But why is what I said so big a deal?"

"You've said it. The damage is done."

Raoul Felder, the divorce lawyer, joined Jackie Mason at the bar. Norman waved to Felder. Felder nearly broke his neck craning it to see us.

Recently, Norman had told me that I was his second wife. To be more accurate I was his seventh wife. Seven years with Norman would make me his common-law wife—in the state of California. By 1991, Norman and I had been together nine years.

After our dinner at the Symphony House, Norman and I returned to our apartment where he signed a galley of *Harlot's Ghost* to my mother. "To Laura, on her 91st. Cheers, dear. Norman." Then he began to sign a galley for me. "To Carole...," he wrote. He put down his pen. Thought. Shuffled his feet. Looked out the window. Cleared his throat. Norman Mailer was at a loss for words, something I never believed was possible.

"I have to finish this at another time," he said.

He never did.

I did not have time to open his novel because I was preparing an interview for *Playboy* between Kurt Vonnegut and Joseph Heller and pursuing the magazine for another assignment.

On May 12th, I had written Christie Hefner, Chairman and CEO of *Playboy*, whom I had met at a business party. I pitched an interview with David Geffen, who had agreed over the phone to be interviewed by me. I had known Geffen from around town, and one afternoon in the mid-eighties I had run into him on the beach in Malibu as he was strolling with, of all people, his friend, Warren Beatty. In May of 1991 Geffen took my call about an interview when he was, ironically, in the dentist's office in New York. He was courteous and witty and agreed to an interview.

A few weeks later Christie Hefner wrote me the following response:

> Dear Carole:
> Thank you for your May 12 letter, your kind words, and your interest in working with us. I would very much like us to continue the dialogue about David Geffen and duo interviews. I will be asking Kevin Buckley to call you since you are both in New York and since you will be able to move all the appropriate arrangements forward. I enjoyed seeing you at the party and look forward to having you in our *Playboy* family of writers.
>
> Regards,
> Christie Hefner

Since David Geffen had agreed to my interview, I told my editor Kevin Buckley at *Playboy*. Then I heard nothing from him. A few months later I opened *Playboy*, and there was an interview with Geffen conducted by a staff writer, which was cheaper for the publication because my fee of $10,000 had been established by the Vonnegut/Heller interview.

Editor Kevin Buckley was married to Gail Lumet, a writer who was published by Knopf, a division of Mailer's publisher, Random House.

Though the Vonnegut/Heller interview was a success, and I received many letters of praise (including one from Diane Sawyer who wrote, "I loved the rap session with the boys…."), I was never published by *Playboy* again. Had Kevin Buckley known Norman was going to end our affair? Had Kevin Buckley whispered to Christie Hefner about my relationship with Norman? Or was I getting paranoid?

Because of the success of my *Esquire* interview, I was invited to many events that celebrities attended. Since I was a freelance journalist, I would try to get the celebrities to agree to an interview and then attach the magazine. But *Playboy* and *Esquire* were the two magazines that paid the most, and my relationship with them was now tarnished. However, there were other magazines. *Penthouse* had given me an assignment for a cover story to interview Dudley Moore in the upcoming months in L.A., and I was able to conduct an interview about sex between Erica Jong and Jay McInerney at the Algonquin. I later sold this piece to *Time Out*. Then Brooke Astor and Reverend Jesse Jackson permitted me to interview them about literacy. In time I sold this to *Hamptons* magazine.

However, while *Penthouse* paid well, the other magazines paid very little. This was not a way to support myself.

During that summer of 1991, because I was on deadline for the Vonnegut/Heller interview for *Playboy*, I stopped taking Norman's many collect calls. I became irritated.

The following message was left on my answering machine. It was in Norman's famous southern accent.

"Listen, Carole, there's no need to go into that grand opera deal about 'a millionaire doesn't have to make collect calls.'" Norman's voice was agitated. "You know perfectly well that you've never lost a cent on a collect call. In fact, you've probably made a small, although not insignificant, profit on them." (Norman's focus on this small amount of money showed his cheap side, like not allowing me to order a side dish of string beans.)

"The reason you didn't hear from me for a few days is that I've been having a hell of a time with the piece on Warren Beatty." It occurred to me that Norman's virtual infatuation with Beatty was getting in the way of his writing the truth.

"I don't want any more of this horseshit. If you don't want to receive my collect calls, we can do without talking to each other all summer. Ciao."

That summer, our calls resumed. Stasis.

In late August after I finished my Vonnegut/Heller interview, I cracked open the galley of *Harlot's Ghost*. Random House finally had sent two copies via messenger. In the margins I scribbled notes about the biographical details that had been fictionalized. I wrote the names of the people who had been put into composites to create Norman's fictional characters. To me, *Harlot's Ghost* was nonfiction—with the names changed. The plot was fiction, but the characters were based on persons I knew. The technique Norman had taught me to use to write a novel.

When I finished my Vonnegut/Heller interview, I drove out to Bridgehampton to see Kurt and Joe who were pleased with my piece, as was *Playboy*. Joe inscribed a copy of *Catch 22*: "To Carole Mallory, Best wishes to a fellow member of the writing game. I enjoyed seeing you again and talking with you for *Playboy*. Joe Heller, August 5, 1991, E. Hampton, NY."

The last time I saw Kurt Vonnegut, he said, "I've written a letter for you. I hope it helps you." He handed me the following:

August 39, 1991

Dear Carole,

Parade did its readers a favor, which is their duty after all, when they turned your biographical sketch into an inspirational piece rather than a book promotion. It must have encouraged a lot of heartbroken people to stop feeling sorry for themselves and get moving again. The blow you suffered, the lobotomization of your once bright and charming father, could not have been more severe. It takes more than courage to survive a horror on that scale. I suggest that you were gifted as well, as an actress and as a keen observer, too, as a potential journalist and social commentator. So, after you tamed your addictions, you could think of all sorts of interesting jobs you could do. Most recovering addicts, once they're clean, are still without a clue as to where they might fit into workaday society. I say you should put together a portfolio after the Heller-Vonnegut thing is published, and ask some magazines for the status of a regular contributor, with their guaranteeing to pay you so and so much each year for so and so many pieces. You not only need such an arrangement, you deserve one.

Cheers,
Kurt Vonnegut

Kurt's letter made me feel valued, appreciated. He was a special man. I loved the date August 39. Wit permeated everything he did, but I wondered why he was so concerned about my future and used the word "need" regarding my ability to earn a living? Did he know something I didn't know about Norman's feelings toward me? Did he know what Norman was about to do?

On September 16, 1991, Norman called from a pay phone. This was the first time all summer he had not called collect.

"Norris has found out about us." His voice was weak. "I've taken a vow not to see you anymore."

I had been kicked. Stabbed. I didn't believe him. He didn't mean it. He'd change his mind tomorrow. He had had a fight with Norris. He couldn't be this cruel. No, not Norman. Now I thought I knew why he called himself Herbert, my father's name. He was deserting me too.

Why was I choosing men who'd enter my life like a shot of amphetamine and who'd leave my life as though I had to be erased? I was angry. No wonder Random House hadn't wanted to send me a galley of *Harlot's Ghost*. Even its PR department had known he was going to make this call.

No wonder Kurt had written that letter. Norman could have told Kurt. They were friends.

Norman's voice was tense. "If I hadn't taken that vow, my marriage would have been broken."

"You took a vow when you married Norris, and you broke it when you met me nine years ago. You've been breaking that vow for years. Don't give me that crap!"

"I have and I don't feel all that good about it—if you want to know the truth."

"Norman, this isn't fair."

"It's not fair, but there it is."

I felt like throwing up.

"Look, Carole, if you don't think it's fair, and you're getting very angry then you'll do something about it. So do it! What can I tell you? Go ahead and blow the whistle and get it over with. You will be totally dead in the media for the simple reason…"

"That you're married, and I'm the dirty one. You're protected."

"Yeah, they'll all dump on you. You'll be viewed as a very bad lady."

"Not everyone sits in judgment on that kind of thing."

"You want to be viewed as a bad lady? Go ahead."

"Sorry, Norman, I try very hard not to base my opinion of myself on what others think of me. You're talking to yourself. Don't expect me to protect your marriage of convenience any longer." My anger surfaced.

"If you're going to run to the papers, go ahead. Automatically you will get bruised far more than I ever will."

"And you'll claim that you've suddenly gotten a conscience and morals when you've been an adulterer for nine years? Your conscience is your bank account."

"My conscience is my business," Norman said angrily. "And so is my marriage. I love Norris."

"What were you doing with me for nine years?"

"That's neither here nor there."

I felt discarded. "Norman, you've told people about us. Our affair isn't secret. Don't try to intimidate me because of your fear of public opinion or the press. The great liberal intellectual caught hiding behind his wife's petticoat. Calling his cowardly deceit 'fidelity.' That's the story for the press. Why did you call me all summer?"

"This happened in the last week. When I called you the other day, she walked into the room. I said, 'I can't talk now.' I was in the middle of the phone call. She caught me." Norman was short of breath.

"Norman, she's known all along about us. You and Norris had an arrangement, and for nine years I was part of it. It's that simple."

"Please deposit five cents for the next five minutes, or your call will be terminated," an operator said. "This is a recording."

Our love had been a recording. Just another married man ending his affair.

"Think what you like," Norman said without feeling. "There was no arrangement."

"I want you to call Mother," I said desperately. "You have an obligation to call a ninety-year-old woman."

"I may call your mother and ask about her health and explain why we had to break up. I'm perfectly willing to do that." Norman never called my mother.

"Why are you being such a weakling and doing this over the phone?" I asked, brushing away my tears.

"Well, I am, aren't I? I mean I can take you to lunch, but there would be a fucking scene in the restaurant that I don't want to contemplate. Besides, you told me you prefer doing things over the phone because when I'm around, you can't think. I'll talk to you early next week."

"I'm leaving town Thursday."

"I hear you. All right."

"Goodbye," I said, wiping away my tears.

This was goodbye. To the man who in 1984 had written, "Some good man is going to treat you right."

This was goodbye. To the man who for nine years had brought ingredients in a Ziploc bag from Brooklyn to Manhattan to teach me how to cook his favorite recipes.

This was goodbye. To the man who for nine years had wanted to hold me like a baby kangaroo in his roly-poly pouch and never let me go.

This was goodbye. To the man who for nine years had begged me to get off caffeine because he cared about my health.

This was goodbye.

I hung up and felt worthless. Running into the bathroom, I sat on the floor, clutched the toilet seat, vomited, and cried. Then I sat up and wiped my mouth with my sleeve.

How could he do this to me? I had given up having a baby by staying with him. I was forty-nine. What had I done with my life? I sat in a corner of the bathroom for a long time. Then I stood up, looked into the mirror, and saw wrinkles and crow's-feet. Nine years ago they weren't there. Jowls were forming. Age was rearing its ugly head. What would happen to me? I saw the stark situation for the first time.

In the living room I gathered most of Norman's writings. In a panic, I decided they had to be put in a safety deposit box. A strange fear of Norman surfaced. I felt that he could try to erase me from his life. After all, his best friend Buzz Farber had been erased. I collapsed on the sofa. I felt uncomfortable. Then I recalled that after Buzz had introduced me to Norman, he went to jail.

I began to tremble. Buzz went to prison for nine years for a crime related to a drug smuggling operation. I read somewhere that some people thought Norman had been an investor.

God, what had I gotten myself involved in? I had to do some research. Nervously, I leafed through stacks of magazines and scanned my books, then I came upon the facts. In November of 1984 a judge had tried Buzz and Dick Stratton, Norman's best friend with whom I thought Norman had a homosexual infatuation. Stratton would not testify against Norman. DEA agents had tried to involve Norman.

I became more frightened. Apparently Buzz had implicated all of them on tapes, but his tapes weren't enough to convict Mailer. There was no actual evidence. Seven and a half metric tons of hash was never seized.

What had happened to this hash? Had it been it sold?

I stood up and went to the window. My stomach felt queasy again. If the hash had been sold, who had that money?

Then I remembered in 1987, when I was on the cover of *Parade,* Norman repeatedly asked me to visit Buzz. "Buzz is despondent," Norman would say. "He's in jail in upstate Pennsylvania. Will you come with me to visit him?"

"Why, Norman, should I drive with you to a jail?"

"Do it for Buzz? He's so sad."

"I never liked Buzz. He was a sexist. You know that. I don't want to be involved with him or Stratton."

"You would be helping me out. We could be together for four hours during the drive. You've overcome so much in your life. Maybe you could give him hope."

"I've never been to a jail in my life and have no intentions of visiting one to please you, Norman. Ask Norris to go."

Then I thought more about Buzz. I sank onto the sofa. After he was released from jail, he was found dead in his car. My heart was pounding as I thought about it. The police report said it was a suicide. Carbon monoxide poisoning.

Norman told me, "Buzz died of a heart attack before the carbon monoxide got to him. He wanted to die that much." How did Norman know this? I wondered if Buzz was supposed to have gotten some of the money from that shipment. I broke out in a cold sweat.

Was there a connection between 1984 when Buzz went to jail and his release in 1991 when Norman ended our affair?

I felt threatened. I stood and looked out the window. People were walking hurriedly by in the street. Would I be able to do that again? To walk with purpose and without fear? My life seemed meaningless. The only meaning it had had was what use Norman could make of me. I began to wonder if I were safe.

How could I have been so naïve?

In 1990, after I became concerned about AIDS, I insisted Norman wear a condom if he wanted to penetrate me.

I was trying to figure out the things that caused the change in our relationship. It must have been something that I took away from our sex life that he needed, which was not consistent with my insisting I be protected. My act of self-affirmation must have changed the relationship because he stopped trying to enter me. Why would my insisting on something that most women in America would consider every day common sense apparently cause him to lose interest in me? It must have had something to do with power and his making me put myself at risk that turned him on. I remembered his definition of love was "being willing to die for." I wasn't willing to die for Norman Mailer. He could have viewed my forcing him to wear a condom as my rejecting him and my challenging his virility. In his vindictive mind, if I rejected him, he was going to reject me and not be my friend. What did I expect? Look how he had reacted to *Esquire*'s cartoon of him kissing Gore. He had raged. *Esquire* had outed his bisexuality, and he had blamed me for it. I did not authorize the cartoon. *Esquire*'s editors had because of the words Norman had chosen to say in the interview.

My God! He had given me trichomonas years before, and I still had not forced him to wear a condom. Where had been my self-worth? I had been naïve and had trusted Norman. He was still a father figure. He reminded me of my father, Herbert, and he did everything in his power to make me feel he was Herbert. Even leaving me notes signed "Herbert" and making collect calls from "Herbert." By keeping this connection to my father alive, he could get me to do anything he wanted.

But my father wouldn't hurt me. My father was a kind and loving man. The only relationship between my father and Norman was the tortured childhood which I suffered at the hands of my father due to his disease. His mental illness made my childhood one of torture. But my suffering was not intentional, on the part of the doctors or my father. My father did not choose to torture me. Norman Mailer was not my father. Norman Mailer was not a kind and loving man. Norman Mailer chose not to wear a condom, which could harm me, kill me. Norman Mailer was a sadist.

I curled up into a fetal position on the sofa. What would I tell my mother? My friends?

What did it matter?

He had given me the gift of all of those writing lessons, but to write alone without conversations with him would be so lonely. I had devoted nine of my best years to Norman. Had I been a fool?

No, I told myself. I had my experiences.

I blew my nose into a Kleenex and rubbed my eyes.

But I was afraid. All kinds of questions occurred to me at once. What would happen to me financially? Norman had promised to leave me in his will or to get an insurance policy for me. I never forced him to honor these commitments. It was obvious that he had never wanted to do these things. He never cared about my well-being. What would happen to me in my old age? Could I support myself? He had been giving me half of my rent each month and had promised to do this for the rest of my life. Now the man who had written *Some Honorable Men* was reneging on his commitment. He had helped introduce me to writers to interview. He had given me confidence in the dog-eat-dog world of journalism. How would I cope?

I dried my eyes, sat up, and looked at Kurt Vonnegut's beautiful letter to me and wondered had Norman told Kurt that he was going to end our affair? Is this why Kurt had written this letter encouraging me to try to get a magazine to hire me as a contributing editor to guarantee me a certain amount of income a month?

After Norman ended our relationship, I began to feel a chill from certain editors. Within the publishing industry, many people knew about our affair. While we were together, Norman and I were accepted. Why this chill when I approached them on my own? I began to feel shunned. I was shunned.

Liz Smith, who championed me in the press, would not talk to me at events. When I was given an assignment from *Mirabella* to interview Liz Smith talking to Governor Ann Richards, Liz Smith refused to grant me the interview. It was to be called "Two Texans." Governor Richards's press secretary had written me a letter stating that "Governor Richards very much enjoys your work and the magazine." He wrote that she agreed to the interview. I needed this interview not only for my résumé, but I needed income, which Liz Smith denied me.

Shortly after our breakup, Harold Evans, who was Norman's publisher, met with me in his office. I wanted to pitch a book. I needed to earn a living. By now I had interviewed: Gore Vidal, Kurt Vonnegut, Joseph Heller, Chevy Chase, Julian Lennon, Isabella Rossellini, Dudley Moore, Baryshnikov, Lord David Puttnam, Milos Forman, Jerry Leiber and Mike Stoller. In 1988 I had published *Flash*. Harold Evans sat a bit close to me in our meeting then said, "Carole, you must understand I say this for your benefit, but for you to publish a book of interviews would not be a good move. If sales are not brisk, and books containing celebrity interviews with a connective narrative do *not* sell well, you will damage your career."

I had the feeling I was listening to a used car salesman. Evans stood and handed me a copy of *Candide*. "It's a little book," he said. I left looking down at the little man.

In 1997, at an event where the paparazzi were eager for photos, I made rabbit ears behind Evans's head as he looked toward the camera. *The Post* published the photo.

Harold Evans was ultimately fired from Random House.

A few weeks after Norman's breakup call, the book party for *Harlot's Ghost* was held. I had been invited by Norman, but this was before he had ended our relationship. I didn't go. Instead I stayed in my apartment and wondered what had happened to us.

Had there been a connection between the publication of Norman's novel and our breakup? Norman was about connections. It occurred to me, not for the first time, that for the entire nine years he had been claiming me as a tax deduction. He had asked me on two separate occasions for my permission to use me as a deduction for two separate years, but had he been deducting me without my permission for the remaining years? Had I been Norman's and Norris's tax deduction titled "research for his novel" and had Norris agreed to allow Norman to have an affair with me until its publication?

Sitting at my desk, I went through my diary that I had kept on our relationship. Norman had told me in 1986 that Norris knew about us. Maybe they had created some kind of game about me. With Mailer's name and sex, their game? Those "swinging" weekends given by multimillionaire John Kluge at his estate in Virginia—Mailer had enjoyed those. The irony was that Norman and Norris spent their summers in Provincetown, known for its homosexual community. Here the gossips referred to Norris as "straight bait." Her beauty attracted men while the gay men appealed to Norman's bisexual side.

I opened the Manso oral biography that Norman had bought me. I read that Norris and Norman liked a good prank. When Norris met Norman's lawyer, Ivan Fisher, and his wife, Norris put on a blonde wig, dressed like a hooker, used an accent, and then went to the ladies room where she changed into an elegant black cocktail dress, took off the wig, and dropped the accent. When she reappeared, the Fishers didn't recognize her. Norris Church was good at playing games.

I didn't feel used just by Norman Mailer; I felt used by Norris Church. But Norman was the one pulling the strings.

I wondered if the divorce lawyer, Raoul Felder, whom we had seen at the Symphony House, had something to do with Norman's ending our affair. Did I have the potential for a palimony suit? Norman had stayed with me intermittently from 1984 to 1987 when he visited Los Angeles. We had had apartments in New York together. If I had been Norman's common-law wife, maybe he had been a bigamist. A lawyer friend told me I had the basis for several lawsuits against Norman. Breach of contract was a big one.

But fighting deep pockets when your pocket was shallow, only made you fodder for the lawyers. Soon dreading the thought, I would have to return to Hollywood and try to settle that fire. Maybe I could recoup some of the value of my possessions, but that settlement was looking doubtful.

I had had a life before Norman. I could find myself again. I would have to accept that I did not know all the rules and would make mistakes. I needed to own up to them and not be ashamed. Norman had taught me to write, but also to be ashamed. Without him, maybe I could find a new freedom.

After all was said and written, I would try to remember the good things.

I was angry. I needed time.

One day I would write about Norman. Try to use the skills he had taught me to bring him to life. But would I ever be able to let go of this anger so I could remember how much I loved him? How it had been in the beginning? All the good things about Norman along with the bad?

No, Gordon Lish had been right. I needed time. "You need seven years before you can write about a subject in nonfiction," Lish would say. "You must be able to dominate your subject. Not be intimidated by him."

By ending our relationship, Norman had done what I had been unable to do. I knew in time I would feel relief. I would let it alone. Not try to see him. Go on with my life. Maybe without Norman in my life things would be less complicated and more good would come my way.

Whenever Norman had been involved in something I was doing, in the beginning his help would be terrific, then suddenly everything would turn sour as it had with *Esquire* and with *Playboy*. I had never understood this. When I reflected upon my nine years with Norman Mailer, I felt as though I had been caught in a revolving door. With the devil.

I thought I understood Norman Mailer, but not all the sinister things he had done to me. It would take years until I could see all of his tricks and schemes and the deceitful web that he had woven and had spun around me. Some of it I will never be able to figure out. I do know there were a lot of fancy money games and that *60 Minutes* was right when it concluded that Norman Mailer was about money. Not liberalism. Not sex. Literature and publicity? Yes, because they generate money.

Then I thought again about Norman's childhood. He would tell me how afraid he had been for his mother. His father had those gambling debts. Trying to collect, criminals would torture his family. Norman lived in fear of never having enough money, right up until his death. It is a paradox that he found comfort while harboring these feelings.

I wondered if that could be why there never was enough of anything for Norman. Women or money. I couldn't help feeling sorry for him when I realized how frightened he had been all of his life. A terrified little boy who longed to feel safe, which meant being in control—regardless of the consequences. Even if this meant harming others.

Norman Mailer made it hard to love Norman Mailer.

Epilogue

When Norman ended our relationship in 1991, I felt as though a limb had been amputated. Gradually over the following ten years, time would heal my cavernous wound.

In September of 1993 I attended an art opening at Christie's and ran into Norman, whom I had not seen since 1991.

"What are you doing here?" I asked him.

"Norris brought me," he said, clutching a drink. "How much did you get out of that fire?"

"None of your business," I said.

"My, aren't we the changed one. You used to tell everyone your secrets. Because of your sobriety." Norman laughed.

"We haven't seen each other for two years, and the first thing you ask about is money! How much did your lawyer friend Ivan Fisher get? He put a claim on my damaged property in to the insurance company then he never took my calls."

"Now, now, let's not squabble. I haven't had a drink for a year and a half." Norman looked down at his glass then held it to the light. "But I'm having one tonight."

"Who's publishing your book on Picasso?" I asked.

"Nan Talese," he said. "Doubleday. There wasn't any trouble with my publisher. That press that Random House was angry with me was trumped up."

I wondered why Norman was justifying his book and his drinking. He appeared to want my approval.

"Did you interview Claude?" I asked.

"No, not yet," Norman said, pushing out his lower lip.

"What's the title?"

"*Picasso, Portrait of an Artist as a Young Man*," he said proudly.

"Terrible title," I said.

"What do you mean?" he said, looking crushed. "But it's about Picasso as a young man." Norman raised his voice.

"So? Call it *Picasso by Mailer*."

"There've been too many books, "*Picasso by....*"

"None by you." Norman liked my point, but didn't change his title.

When I thought about Claude Picasso and Norman Mailer, the two great loves in my life, I realized that the last time I saw Claude was like when we first met, but the last time I saw Norman was nothing like when we first met. In 1993, he was asking my opinion instead of me asking his.

My friend, Bettina Cirone, quickly snapped a photo. I suspected Norman asked about the money I had gotten from the fire because he wanted to know if I had enough money to live on, or if I were going to try to sue him for breach of contract or bigamy. Oh, I did contact civil and criminal lawyers, who, I believe, sent my documents to Norman in an attempt to extort money in exchange for not pursuing my case. Then I gave up.

In 1993, I was invited to the inauguration of President Clinton as a member of the press. This was an exciting honor, but since I did not have a magazine for which to write, I did not know how to turn this experience into income, which I needed.

From 1994 until 2001, my mother lived with me in New York. I stopped writing and focused on caring for her. Having the honor and privilege to care for my mother was the most important thing I have done with my life. During those years, I realized why Norman had wanted to know how much money my mother had. He was planning his exit. He had been here before.

For Mother, I tried to make New York fun. I took her to the theater, the Statue of Liberty, Staten Island, Lincoln Center, Central Park for picnics, the Circle Line, taxi rides, bus rides. After 1996, we did these things with her in a wheelchair. Two strokes had crippled her.

Not fun were the thefts we suffered. Our apartment was burglarized twice.

Norman's property had been stolen. Not all of it, but a good portion. I had had twenty-three inscribed books. Because I was proud of these inscriptions, fortunately I had Xeroxed them. The thieves left me three books. They also left me seventy-eight taped phone conversations. They must not have realized that Norman's voice was on them.

What frightened me most was that statements from our brokerage firm were lying on my desk. They had *not* been there when we left the apartment for lunch. What did the thieves want with these statements? What use could they make of them? The thieves had been able to get account numbers. I was never able to figure out that connection.

In 1999, shortly after the final burglary, I moved to suburban Philadelphia with my cat and my ninety-nine-year-old mother who was wheelchair bound and blind in one eye. Home. Mother and I could face her final years in peace.

In the spring of 2000, I returned to meetings of recovering alcoholics in Flourtown, Pennsylvania, where I met a handsome Italian named Kenneth Gambone. He had a sturdy nose, thick lips, black hair, and big brown eyes. Looking at him brought back all those years I had studied the majesty of Pre-Renaissance art. He had no pretentious literary airs, was a member of the working class, and was the complete opposite of a bourgeois Norman Mailer, who used his keen understanding of the English language to manipulate and to deceive.

Kenny needed a ride home from a meeting. When he got out of the car, he kissed me on the lips, and I fell in love. Again. His kiss was the most sensual I had ever experienced. His touch was magical and comforting. But he was twenty-six years younger than me. Just a flirtation, I told myself. A break from caretaking. For eight years I had been unable to leave my mother unattended without hiring a nurse's aide. By now she was bedridden. Changing her diapers was my daily duty.

Kenny and I began dating. That is, he came over to my mother's apartment and kept us company. After mother went to sleep in her bedroom, Kenny and I would make love in her living room. When I was unable to move mother, Kenny would carry her. Kenny was a great help to mother and to me.

When mother went to heaven in 2001, she was looking at Kenny.

One month after Laura Lulu Lengel Wagner died at age one hundred, Kenneth Gambone, age thirty-two, and I, age fifty-nine, were married. The plan had been for mother to give me away from her wheelchair. She couldn't wait.

Marriage to Kenny Gambone was refreshing after nine years of Norman Mailer. Kenny was real. No schemes. No tricks. Kenny filled the void I felt in losing Norman. Kenny allowed me to care for him as he cared for me. With our two cats and toy poodle we formed a new family.

After being married for five years, Kenny had the idea that Norman and I should be friends.

"You should call him, Carole," Kenny said.

"No," I said.

"Then *I'll* write him," Kenny said. Kenny was terribly Italian. There was no way of dissuading him. When he had an idea, he pursued it.

In 2003, Norman and Kenny began corresponding and soon were having phone conversations. Kenny entertained the thought of meeting Norman, though I tried to talk him out of it. The three of us planned a rendezvous in New York.

In one conversation while Kenny was at the gym, Norman said to me, "I can come down from Provincetown to meet you, but I only want to see you, Carole. We could meet at a hotel in Times Square."

"No, Norman," I said, "I won't see you without Kenny. I'm a married woman, and I love my husband." I hung up on him. Same old Norman. I had told Kenny not to contact him.

I told Kenny that Norman had cancelled the trip due to his writing schedule.

One day in the spring of 2005, I received another peculiar phone call. A voice whispered, "I can be over in one hour. Norris is going out."

"Norman, is that you?" I asked. He must be losing it, I thought.

"Oh, I dialed the wrong number," Norman said in a high voice, one that he frequently used when he lied. He laughed. (I wondered if Norman had really wanted to talk to me, and this was his way of doing it.)

"How are you?" I asked.

"Busy writing," he said. "How are you?"

"I don't write anymore."

"You should not stop writing. With your life? Your experiences?"

"Norman, your interest in my writing was just a ploy for you to use me."

"No, it wasn't. You're a good writer when you set your mind to it. When you stop drinking that caffeine. You must take your time when you write. Caffeine makes you miss moments. Throws off the rhythm."

"What do you care?"

"And stop that preaching. Set scenes. Your scene writing is good. Don't get all slipshod. "

"You treated me badly."

"Have it your way. You always do." Norman paused. "What do you look like today?"

"Older."

"We haven't seen each other for fifteen years. I hope you're showing your forehead and not wearing that sheepdog hairdo."

"Why would you care what I look like?"

"You look so regal with your forehead showing. We had some good fucks in the old days, didn't we?"

"I liked to think we made love, Norman." I paused then said, "I've got to go."

This was my last conversation with Norman. No more tears. I felt bad that Norman had trouble admitting that he loved someone. Though he was a wordsmith, he still used the word "fuck" instead of the word "love." This made me feel diminished. While he had helped me with my writing, I questioned what he had done to my self-worth. What had he thought of my worth? What had I thought of my own worth to have allowed him to treat me the way he did? Those days were over.

I looked at a photo of Kenny and thought how much better my life was without Norman. Kenny had freed me from my obsession with him. I had been trapped and under Norman's spell. Then I no longer thought of Norman Mailer.

Early in 2007, I heard from a friend that Norman was in poor health and could be dying. By now my anger with Norman had faded and turned to gratitude. Our relationship had been not only about sex but about love of the written word. He had taught me a great deal, and I had come to realize that he needed Norris Church to feel whole. She had given her life to him. I had been wrong to judge her so harshly.

Aware that these could be Norman's final days, I called him in Provincetown to say goodbye.

A male secretary answered the phone.

"Is Norman in?" I asked.

"He's out," the secretary said.

"How is he?" I asked.

"Oh, he's doing all right. He's at lunch with a friend."

"Would you tell him that Carole Mallory called? I just wanted him to know that I always loved him."

"I'll give him the message," the secretary said with enthusiasm.

When I hung up, I knew that was the end of all ties to Norman Mailer. While I was sad that a part of my life had ended, it felt good to be able to arrive at the here and now without a ball and chain tugging at my heart. I would be forced to take responsibility for my choices and would be free of a voice of criticism that had dogged me for nine years. This freedom felt good. When Norman had edited my work, there were times when his shouting had hurt deeply. That thick skin he had wanted me to develop with others, I had never quite developed with his criticism of me and my writing. For nine years I felt I had deserved his harsh words. But now I knew that I hadn't. I had my own worth. I had become independent after all those years. This had been a struggle, but finally felt, oh, so good. Furthermore I now had my own husband to love, to care for, to make me happy, and to be good to me, but I would not become dependent on him as I had become on Norman Mailer.

On November 13 of 2007, as I was driving, my cell rang.

"Carole, Norman Mailer just died," Kenny said.

"I had been expecting this," I said.

"What are you doing?"

"Going for a manicure."

"Are you going to come home?"

"What for? He died for me a long time ago."

"I understand," Kenny said.

Norman Mailer died from kidney failure, which often is a result of chronic alcoholism. The keepers of his flame had gotten their way. With each party and macho drinking charade, they had been sealing the nails around his coffin. I had tried to help Norman and had asked him not to drink around me. He did not want to drink when he was with me, but I was not with him constantly. Besides, his body had had years of alcoholic abuse.

No, Norman wanted to drink. He wanted his enablers around him. He needed their approval because he didn't approve of himself. He was filled with self-loathing. "You don't know how bad I am," he would repeat. But I did. He had been an alcoholic, just like me. Except that in 1980 I had stopped drinking and was now sober. Because of this, I was alive. This day.

I cried and thought, *Tragic Norman. He wouldn't let me love him. He had chosen them and alcohol.*

Then I felt relief as though a weight had been lifted from my pen. From my life. Maybe now I could write. I was grateful that I had made that last call. I had wanted to go to Norman's funeral, but realized this was an absurd thought as I walked into the manicurist's salon. Having my manicure was more important than living in the past. Having my nails filed brought me into the now. Norman's suffering was over. So was mine.

Shortly after Norman's death, Kenny said to me, "You have an archive with all those papers you've been carting around all these years. Why don't you see if a university is interested in them?"

Because of Kenny Gambone, I found the courage to call the curators of the libraries of the University of Texas, the New York Public Library, and Harvard University, who all wanted my material. Curators from Harvard University and the New York Public Library came to my home to inspect my collection, but it was Leslie Morris, curator of the Houghton Library at Harvard, Mailer's alma mater, who saw the most worth in my archive. I needed my archive to go to Harvard to set the literary record straight. I needed my archive to go to Harvard to prove to the world that not only had Norman Mailer taught me to write, but I also had been a valuable sober influence on him. I needed my archive to go to Harvard to prove that I had written my own work and that his edits were, indeed, just that.

I valued my work and wanted it placed in an institution with a strong academic reputation where it would be held in high esteem.

Over offers from Tom Staley of the University of Texas and Isaac Gewirtz of the New York Public Library, on February 20, 2008, I chose Harvard University as the home for my archive and became a part of history.

But my greatest accomplishment was the sense of peace I felt with Kenny Gambone and our new family. Now that Norman was dead, I felt that I could live again. Not with celebrity or in bustling New York City or in flashy Hollywood, but deep in suburban Philadelphia. We lived in Valley Forge, Pennsylvania, where George Washington had spent many a winter, and the National Forest was a mile away. Tall trees, deer, rolling fields of grass, and the silence of the countryside became a part of our life. We lunched at simple, inexpensive restaurants and took side trips to New Hope, where Washington had crossed the Delaware, and to haunted Gettysburg, also steeped in history. There were no press parties, no paparazzi, no literary pretensions, nothing to remind me of my past life, and this felt good. I made new friends and went back to meetings in Flourtown, which has a wonderfully supportive group of spiritual beings.

Here celebrities were heard, but not seen, nature was worshipped, and anonymity was a new form of respect.

Serenity had finally come into my life.

Acknowledgments

I want to thank Dr. Catherine Quinn Kearns for her weekly critique of my work, Mary Dearborn for her wise editorial guidance, my patient and gentle agent Irene Webb, my brilliant editor-in-chief Dan Smetanka who encouraged constant soul-searching, and my sister, Elmira Batson, for her tolerance. I'm also grateful to Dr. Lee Dante, Phyllis Butler, Helen Griffin-Shelley, Elise Capron, Leslie Morris, and the late Michael Viner.